Contents

Acknowledgements

This research was commissioned by the Learning and Skills Development Agency (LSDA) with funding support from the Learning and Skills Council. The Youth Cohort Study and Labour Force Survey data were made available by the ESRC Data Archive at the University of Essex. The Pupil Level Annual School Census and National Pupil Database data were supplied by the Department for Education and Skills.

The research was undertaken between April and July 2005 and was managed and supported by Darshan Sachdev, Research Manager at LSDA. The literature review undertaken by Nicholas Houghton was supported by Rosie Zwart, Researcher at LSDA, who carried out the literature searches at different phases of this study.

Grateful thanks are extended to the members of the advisory group for their useful feedback at phases one and two of this study, and to the discussants and the participants of the expert seminar for their helpful comments and suggestions (please see the Appendix for the full list). The feedback received during the first two stages of the study and that received during the expert seminar has proved invaluable in shaping and finalising this report. The views and interpretations of the data presented here, however, are the author's own.

Steven McIntosh
London School of Economics and Political Sciences

Executive summary

Key messages

- The under-achievement of black pupils is more likely to begin earlier, between the ages of 11 and 14, than for white pupils, especially boys, whose under-achievement becomes more apparent between the ages of 14 and 16.

- Social deprivation appears to have a greater effect on the educational performance of white pupils than any other ethnic group.

- Parental interest, such as attendance at parents' evenings, careers advice at school and work experience appear to be some of the key factors which lessen the impact of truancy – used as an indicator of disengagement – on the acquisition of five good GCSEs.

- Of those truants who fail to get five or more good GCSEs, the presence of these factors – supportive parents, careers advice and work experience while at school – is also more likely to lead to participation in further education, especially vocational qualifications.

- While a good background and supportive family increase the chances of a low-achieving individual re-engaging in further education, for the more seriously disengaged these factors are unlikely to have an effect.

- Vocational qualifications have a significant impact on the wages of those who leave school with no qualifications; a Level 2 vocational qualification raises the wages of a previously unqualified school-leaver to the level received by an individual with five good GCSEs from school.

- Previously unqualified young people who acquire vocational qualifications will improve their occupational standing, as well as their wages and employment likelihood. Furthermore, they are not more likely to end up in low-quality (part-time if not actively sought, temporary or short-term jobs) than individuals who have already reached Levels 2 or 3 through their school qualifications.

Introduction

This report brings together a number of strands in one study, and aims to tell a continuous story of those who have disengaged from the education process, from their time at school, through further education and into their working lives.

In this study, disengagement is defined as partial or full withdrawal from the education process, either in terms of attendance or of effort. It is worth noting that the focus is on those who disengage because of disaffection with the education process or their learning, and not on those who have had to disengage from education because of, for example, family problems or caring duties.

The study used large national data sets – representative of the whole population – to supplement evidence from case studies, and aimed to identify who the disengaged are, what effect their disengagement has had on their school examination outcomes, how many re-engage with education by participating in post-compulsory education – and what the characteristics are of those who do – how successful they are in post-compulsory education, and the impact of this continued learning on their labour market outcomes.

The project is in part a scoping study, as it set out to investigate whether such analysis is possible with existing national data sets.

The most relevant information in a national data set that could be found was given in answer to a question in the Youth Cohort Study, asking respondents whether they had played truant during the final year of compulsory schooling, and if so, how frequently.

Individual characteristics associated with under-achievement in Key stage test results

Exploration of data on the whole population of school pupils, including information on their Key stage test results sets the scene for the subsequent analyses. The analysis began with an investigation of who under-achieves during compulsory schooling.

Under-achievement at a particular Key stage is defined here as scoring one standard deviation below the average score of those who obtained the same score as another pupil at the previous Key stage. At Key stage 4 (GCSE), under-achievement can be further defined as scoring below average as just defined, *plus* failing to acquire five or more GCSEs at Grades A*–G.

In the raw data, at Key stage 3, under-achievement on the basis of Key stage 2 results is most common among:

- boys
- Afro-Caribbean black pupils
- African black pupils
- other black pupils
- Bangladeshi pupils
- those entitled to free school meals
- those with special educational needs.

At Key stage 4, under-achievement on the basis of Key stage 3 results is most common among:

- boys (with the gender difference increasing)
- other black pupils
- white British pupils
- mixed-race pupils
- those entitled to free school meals
- those with special educational needs.

There is therefore some evidence that for black pupils who under-achieve the process begins between the ages of 11 and 14 (Key stages 2 and 3), whereas the decline sets in for white pupils – boys in particular – between the ages of 14 and 16 (Key stages 3 and 4).

When looking at the under-achievement at Key stage 3 relative to test scores at Key stage 2, the results from analysis suggest that:

- The highest rate of under-achievement is among Afro-Caribbean black pupils. However, the gap relative to white pupils is smaller than in the raw data, suggesting that some of the poor performance of this group represents a failure to control for social background, which appears to influence under-achievement.

- Girls are slightly less likely to under-achieve than boys.

- The negative impact of free school meals entitlement on Key stage 3 performance is lessened among Indian, Pakistani, Bangladeshi, Afro-Caribbean black, African black and other black pupils.

Looking at under-achievement at Key stage 4 on the basis of Key stage 3 test results show that:

- Under-achievement is greater among boys than girls, with the gap widening after Key stage 3.

- White British pupils, Afro-Caribbean black pupils and other black pupils now have the highest rate of under-achievement of all ethnic groups, while Indian, Pakistani, Bangladeshi and other Asian pupils have the lowest rate, particularly among girls in the first three cases. When attention is focused on under-achievers who fail to obtain five GCSEs at any grade, it is white pupils who are most likely to fall into this category.

- Under-achievement is on average higher among individuals entitled to free school meals. This is particularly so for white pupils, with the performance of other ethnic groups being much less affected by social deprivation.

Looking for under-achievement at Key stage 4 relative to performance at Key stage 2, only for those who under-achieved at Key stage 3, allows us to investigate which of the under-achieving groups at age 14 get their studies back on track by getting the Key stage 4 results predicted by their Key stage 2 marks. The results suggest that those most likely to get back on track are:

- girls

- most of the Asian ethnic groups, and in particular girls in these groups.

Being from a socially disadvantaged background damages the prospects of white pupils getting their studies back on track more than for most other ethnic groups.

Disengagement: truancy in the Youth Cohort Study

The relevant data sets were then examined to identify the characteristics of individual pupils who are most likely to report playing truant from school in Year 11. In the raw data, self-reported truancy rates are highest among:

- girls, somewhat surprisingly, perhaps reflecting their greater honesty rather than their greater truancy, given the results in official records

- black pupils, followed by white pupils, with Asian pupils having the lowest rates

- those with parents (particularly the father) in non-professional jobs

- those not living with both parents (particularly where the mother is absent).

Investigating the factors associated with truancy behaviour through multivariate analysis, the results revealed that:

- Girls *report* a higher truancy rate than boys, somewhat surprisingly, given official administrative data that suggests the opposite.
- After controlling for family background, white pupils have a higher truancy rate than other ethnic groups, although the differences are small.
- Individuals with one of their parents, especially the mother, missing; individuals with parents, particular the father, in non-professional occupations; and individuals living in a rented home, are all more likely to play truant.
- Compared to pupils in comprehensive schools, those in independent and grammar schools report less truancy.
- If individuals receive careers advice in school, or, in particular, if they receive work experience, they are less likely to play truant.
- Whatever an individual pupil's own social background, the higher the proportion of pupils entitled to free school meals in his or her school, the more likely is that individual pupil to play truant himself/herself. This suggests that there may be a peer-group effect on truancy behaviour.

The initial post-compulsory education experiences of former school truants

The relationship between disengagement (truancy) and GCSE performance was explored next, followed by an examination of the characteristics of those former truants who did not achieve well at GCSE but who subsequently re-engage in education and attend further education, and how well they do. Looking first at GCSE performance, the results reveal that:

- Individuals who truanted in Year 11 at school are less likely to acquire five or more Grade A*–C GCSEs, or five or more Grade A*–G GCSEs.
- This effect remains after controlling for background characteristics.
- There is a higher likelihood of success for females, Asian pupils, those from good socio-economic backgrounds, those living with their mother, those who attended independent or grammar schools, those with fewer pupils with special educational needs (SEN) or entitled to free school meals in their school, those who had careers advice or work experience in Year 11, those without SEN themselves and those with supportive parents.

In the year after the completion of compulsory education, those who truanted and failed to achieve five or more good GCSEs at school are:

- less likely to still be in full-time education
- more likely to be in a job
- more likely to be in government training
- much more likely to be unemployed
- more likely to be outside the labour market altogether.

If they truanted and failed to obtain five GCSEs at *any* grade, their economic position is even worse on average, with lower education participation rates and higher unemployment and inactivity rates.

Some former truants who failed to pass five or more good GCSEs nevertheless participate in post-compulsory education. They are more likely to do so if they:

- are female
- are from a non-white ethnic background
- have a higher socio-economic status
- live with (at least) their mother
- had careers interviews and work experience at school
- attended a school with fewer pupils with SEN or entitled to free school meals
- have supportive parents.

Most of these impacts are the same for very low-achievers who fail to obtain five GCSEs at *any* grade, or for pupils with serious truancy behaviour, with the exception that many of the social background indicators have a negligible impact on the re-engagement probabilities of these more disengaged groups.

The next question for investigation was what individuals study if they participate in post-compulsory education. The results suggest that:

- Non-disengaged pupils at school are most likely to take A-levels if they remain in post-compulsory education.
- Among former truants who failed to achieve five or more good GCSEs, very few do A-levels after compulsory education. While some do GCSE retakes, the most popular option, if learning is continued, is to study for vocational qualifications.

Concentrating on such vocational qualifications from this point on, the analysis then looked at the characteristics associated with studying for a vocational qualification. Among former truants, characteristics associated with vocational learning are similar to those associated with full-time education in general. Therefore, those more likely to study for vocational qualifications among former truants are:

- females
- those from a non-white ethnic background
- those from a higher socio-economic status (though becoming less important than when explaining participation in full-time education in general)
- those who live with (at least) their mother
- those who had careers interviews and work experience at school
- those who attended a school with fewer pupils with SEN
- those with supportive parents.

Data sets were then examined to identify how well individuals succeed in further education. The results show that:

- Former truants who failed to acquire at least five good GCSEs are very unlikely to obtain A-levels in the two years following completion of compulsory schooling.

- Only small numbers of this group acquire GCSEs through resits during this period.

- Significant numbers – up to about half – of all former low-achieving truants, however, reach Level 2 via vocational qualifications over the same time period.

- Of the very low-achieving former truants, very few (about 15%) acquire any vocational qualifications during this period.

Finally, considering the characteristics of those who succeed in re-engaging and acquiring a post-compulsory vocational qualification, the results show that very few factors are significantly associated with former low-achieving truants nevertheless achieving Level 2 via vocational qualifications. Analyses suggest a higher likelihood of such achievement for:

- females

- non-white ethnic groups (tentatively, given a lack of statistical significance)

- those from a higher socio-economic background (though this factor appears much less important than it was in explaining, for example, GCSE attainment earlier)

- those still living with at least one parent

- those without SEN

- those with supportive parents.

The relationship between vocational qualifications and labour market outcomes

Earlier analyses showed that a significant number of those who played truant – and who failed to achieve five or more good GCSEs – nevertheless acquire some vocational qualifications after the end of compulsory schooling. Data sets were then examined to investigate whether the acquisition of vocational qualifications is worthwhile in terms of improved labour market outcomes.

The Labour Force Survey data set was used, because of its detailed information on labour market outcomes. However, as it does not ask questions about truancy at school, former truants cannot be identified. The analysis therefore divided the sample according to the level of school qualifications they achieved, with most of the analysis focusing on those who did not acquire any vocational qualifications (which will probably include many of the former disengaged pupils, but will also include other such individuals who did not succeed at school for other reasons). The analysis focused on British-born people in their twenties at the time of their inclusion in the survey.

The first set of results looked at the distribution of school-level qualification acquisition, and showed that:

- a significant minority of young people continue to leave school with no qualifications

- the achievement of girls is slightly better than that of boys.

Considering qualification acquisition after completing compulsory schooling, it was found that:

- The majority of both young men and women who get no qualifications at school also do not obtain any qualifications after school.

- If pupils acquire post-school qualifications, they are most likely to be at Level 1; only one in three manage to reach Level 2, and one in six reach Level 3.

- Individuals who acquired qualifications at school are also more likely to obtain qualifications after leaving school, most typically at one level above their highest school qualification.

Further analyses examined how the acquisition of post-compulsory qualifications affects individuals' labour market outcomes, separately for each level of school qualification acquisition. Looking first at the likelihood of employment, the following results emerged.

- For unqualified school-leavers, the acquisition of vocational qualifications is strongly associated with higher employment rates.

- For men, a vocational qualification at Levels 2 or 3 virtually closes the employment probability gap relative to those who reached these levels via school-based academic qualifications (five or more good GCSEs and A-levels respectively), while for women the gap is closed considerably.

- For men, there is little change in the probability of employment with vocational qualification acquisition compared with those who acquire qualifications at school. For women, employment likelihoods continue to rise with vocational qualification acquisition, albeit at a falling rate, for levels of school achievement all the way up to, and including, the five or more GCSE A*–C group. Only those women who achieved A-levels at school do not gain any benefit from acquiring vocational qualifications, in terms of their employment likelihood.

With respect to the part-time/full-time classification of jobs, the following patterns emerge.

- Among men, there is no evidence of any statistically significant relationship between qualification acquisition and the likelihood of working part-time. This is principally because, overall, only small numbers of men work in part-time jobs.

- Many more women work in part-time jobs, and the evidence suggests that those with no qualifications at all are most likely to perform such jobs. Beyond that, however, among young women with some qualifications, there is little evidence of a systematic relationship between further qualification acquisition and the likelihood of working part-time.

For jobs with permanent/temporary status, it was found that:

- There is little evidence for a relationship between individuals' qualifications and their likelihood of working in a job that is temporary for some reason.

- The strongest association is that individuals with HE qualifications are more likely to work in temporary jobs.

With respect to job tenure, the analysis shows that:

- There is no relationship between qualifications acquired and months of tenure in current job, with the exception of shorter tenure among those with HE qualifications, for the simple reason that they will have spent less time on the labour market.

Vocational qualification acquisition, however, has an impact on the level of job performed, as analyses showed that:

- The acquisition of post-school vocational qualifications is associated with unqualified male school-leavers moving up the occupation hierarchy from elementary and unskilled/semi-skilled manual occupations into skilled manual occupations. Only if they acquire an HE qualification, however, do these men break into senior non-manual occupations in significant numbers.

- Similar effects are observed for men who leave school with fewer than five good GCSEs, while for those with good school-leaving qualifications, significant numbers work in senior occupations even when they hold no post-school qualifications, and so the influence of vocational qualifications on the occupation structure of such individuals is smaller.

- Unqualified female school-leavers are most likely to work in administrative, personal service, sales and elementary occupations. As they acquire vocational qualifications, they move away from the latter two occupation groups, and into the former two. Unlike for men, very few move into skilled manual jobs.

- Similar patterns are observed for women who left school with some, but fewer than five, good GCSEs, with the exception that higher numbers with no post-school qualifications work in administrative occupations, but this proportion does not change as post-school vocational qualifications are acquired.

- For women who leave school with five or more good GCSEs or with A-levels, the acquisition of post-school vocational qualifications has virtually no impact on their occupation structure, and it is only HE qualifications that get such women into senior non-manual occupations.

There is also an impact on wages and results suggest that:

- Vocational qualifications have a significant impact on the wages of those who left school with no qualifications, but little impact on the wages of those who acquired qualifications at school.

- A Level 2 vocational qualification raises the wages of a previously unqualified school-leaver to the level received by an individual with Level 2 GCSEs from school. The wage return attached to a Level 3 vocational qualification, however, cannot match that attached to acquiring A-levels at school.

Finally, the specific qualifications with the largest impact on labour market outcomes (improving employability, occupational status and wages) – for both men and women – seem to be NVQs (though not at Level 1). In addition, apprenticeships and City and Guilds qualifications at Advanced Craft level seem to have had an impact for men only.

In *summary*, the acquisition of vocational qualifications can be beneficial for individuals who have failed at school but re-entered education in further education, in terms of better labour market prospects, particularly greater employability, higher job status and higher earnings. The challenge is therefore to increase the number of low-achievers from school re-entering education (or training) and acquiring such qualifications, since at present only a minority of those who leave school without qualifications obtain them after leaving school.

1 | Introduction

1
Source: DfES website,
Trends in Education
and Skills available via
www.dfes.gov.uk/trends/
upload/xls/5_5t.xls (chart a).

The level of achievement in British schools has risen substantially over the last 20 years or so. Many more schoolchildren now acquire qualifications at the end of compulsory schooling than used to be the case. In 1998–9, 33% of those completing compulsory schooling acquired five or more GCSEs at Grade C or above, whereas by 2003–4 this figure was 54%.[1] However, there still remains a group of pupils who do not successfully complete lower secondary schooling. 'Successfully' in this context can mean a failure to reach a given standard that is the same for all pupils (such as the commonly used 'five or more GCSEs at Grades A*–C), or a failure to reach one's own targets, aims or potential, and thus under-achieve in a personal sense.

There will be many reasons why individual pupils might be unsuccessful in either or both of these ways. A key reason for a lack of success, particularly relative to the five or more good GCSE benchmark, will be natural ability. Not everyone is capable of reaching this benchmark, and if everyone was able to achieve it, it would soon be protested that the benchmark is too easy to achieve and not sufficiently challenging.

Other reasons could include problems at home, having to devote time away from studying towards caring for family members, or towards working part-time to earn money for the individual themselves or their family. For each of these reasons, the pupil could be said to have disengaged from the education process, in order to perform the other duties or try to solve (or escape from) the family problems. In many of these circumstances, therefore, the disengagement may have been forced on the individual, who did not necessarily choose their own course of action. Still, they are not participating, either fully or perhaps at all, in the education process, and so from the point of view of education, and only education, they can be thought of as disengaged (they are not necessarily disengaged from society as a whole – the person who spends time away from school to care for a relative could be thought of as a very dedicated member of society).

Another reason, however, for disengagement from the education process could be disaffection with schools, learning and education in general. It is this type of disengagement that is the primary focus of this research, to study those who have become so uninterested in their own education that they no longer participate, either fully or at all, and thus for whom disengagement has been a deliberate choice.

Scope of the research

Various aspects of this particular type of disengagement were examined in the research study. In particular, the study was designed to identify the characteristics of such individuals, to build up a picture of them. To the extent that knowledge can be obtained about these characteristics, it should be possible to predict who is particularly vulnerable to disengagement, so that possible intervention could be undertaken that may deflect such individuals from such a course in the future. One possible means of persuasion could be a detailed presentation of the consequences of such disengagement, and so knowledge of such consequences is also important. Finally, it is necessary not to give up on previously disengaged pupils who are adults today. It would be useful, therefore, to know how such individuals can still participate in learning after the completion of compulsory schooling, what their chances of success in such learning are, and what impact such learning would have on the rest of their lives, and in particular their labour market outcomes. Knowledge of such outcomes, if positive, could then be used to persuade previously disengaged pupils to re-engage in learning. This then completes the definition of the research questions to be addressed here.

The original specification of this research project was as a scoping study, to see how far the research questions posed above could be answered using large, national data sets. Much previous work on the correlates, consequences and solutions to disengagement has been based upon the analysis of small groups of individuals who are either vulnerable to disengagement or have already disengaged, often using informal discussions to obtain information, rather than following a rigid questionnaire. Such research is vital to fully understand individuals' circumstances, their thoughts and their reasoning for potentially or actually disengaging from education. A weakness in such methodology is that any results obtained can have no claim to generalisability to the population as a whole, and are specific to the group of individuals who participated in the study.

The analysis of large-scale data sets, on the other hand, can provide estimates of the parameters of the relationships being investigated that are relevant for the population as a whole, thus quantifying the causes and consequences of disengagement through the use of appropriate statistical techniques applied to nationally representative data sets. Such research therefore provides the bigger picture and expresses the average relationships that hold in the population as a whole, though of course missing some of the individual-specific details that are obtained through careful case studies. Thus the two research methodologies are mutually supportive. As mentioned above, since much of the work on disengagement from education is of the case study variety, the principal aim of this research was to see to what extent existing large, national data sets can contribute to the disengagement literature.

Defining key concepts

The use of large, national data sets for this project meant that useable definitions of the key concepts had to be found within them, and indeed the original motivation for the project was to investigate whether existing data sets provided any information of use for creating such definitions. As described above, under-achievement, for example, can be defined in terms of a failure to reach a set benchmark such as five good GCSEs, or in terms of a failure to achieve one's potential. Many existing data sets contain questions asking respondents to report their qualifications, and so obtaining data on who achieves the GCSE benchmark is not difficult. Less straightforward is the other aspect of under-achievement, namely, failure to achieve one's potential, given that potential is a very difficult concept to obtain reliable data upon.

The data set chosen was an administrative data set on all pupils in the country (the merged Pupil Level Annual School Census (PLASC) and National Pupil Database (NPD)data set). The benefit of this data set is that it contains results of tests taken by pupils throughout their school careers, and so potential can be defined in terms of performance on earlier tests, and under-achievement in terms of failing to meet the standards set in earlier tests. In addition, final outcomes in terms of GCSE results are also contained in the data set, and so the absolute benchmark definition of under-achievement can, and will, also be used.

As for disengagement, and specifically disengagement caused by disaffection with schools or learning, after an examination of available national data sets, it was concluded that the truancy variable in the Youth Cohort Study (YCS) represented the best available indicator of disengagement. This variable asks respondents to report how often they played truant in the final year of compulsory schooling.

In *summary*, under-achievement will be measured either absolutely by the failure to achieve five or more good GCSEs (or five GCSEs at any grade), or relatively by the failure to match one's performance at a previous Key stage in one's school career (or both). Disengagement caused by disaffection will be measured by the frequency of one's truancy (if any).

Before continuing, a few points must be made about these definitions. The key point is that they were chosen not because they perfectly capture the concepts we are attempting to measure, but because they are the most appropriate available in large, national data sets in the UK, which were to be the information source for this project, as described above. Thus it is not being argued that truancy is the only manifestation of disaffected disengagement, nor that truancy necessarily even reflects disengagement. For example, in the first case, a pupil who continues to attend school all of the time, but daydreams constantly through classes and submits no work could be thought of as having disengaged from the education process, but of course would not show up in truancy statistics.

Similarly, in the second case, a young person who occasionally misses school to attend to some caring duties, looking after a sick or handicapped parent or sibling for example, but does their utmost to catch up on the work missed, should not be thought of as having disengaged from the education process, but would nevertheless show up in truancy data. Even if they were to give up on their studies because of their other responsibilities, and thus be said to have disengaged, this is not primarily the sort of disengagement that is the focus of this study, since such individuals were not disaffected with their studies, but had to disengage to devote their energies elsewhere.

Unfortunately, the YCS does not ask what individuals were doing when they truanted, and so it is not possible to identify those who truanted because they were disengaged and disaffected, those who were disengaged but not through choice and not because they were disaffected, and those who were not really disengaged at all if they were continuing their studies and learning outside school. Thus truancy is not an ideal measure of disaffected disengagement, but it will be used simply out of necessity, as it seemed to be the variable most closely related to disengagement available in large, national data sets. Its appropriateness can in some ways be judged by the results it produces. If the final results are plausible – given that truancy is supposed to be indicating disengagement – then this would provide the truancy variable with some validity. Ultimately, however, it must be borne in mind that the results refer to self-reported truancy, and not a more direct measure of disengagement.

A second point to make clear is that under-achievement and disengagement are two separate concepts. Under-achievement is a possible consequence of disengagement, and this relationship will be investigated in this report. However, it is not being claimed that under-achievement and disengagement are the same thing, nor that disengagement is the only cause of under-achievement. Many pupils will under-achieve due to some of the reasons listed above, even though they continued with their learning and exerted effort in their studies. However, for this research report, the focus is not going to be on these other reasons, but on disengagement (as measured by the truancy variable).

A third point to make is that the data to be used in this project is cross-sectional in nature, and so strictly speaking can reveal a relationship such as one between disengagement and under-achievement, but cannot prove causation from one to the other, in this case in the hypothesised direction from disengagement to under-achievement. In fact, the causal link could actually be the reverse, with failure in exams leading individuals to lose confidence and withdraw from full participation in education. Similarly, there may be no true causal relationship at all between disengagement and under-achievement in either direction; both may be the outcomes of other variables such as low ability, special needs, problems at home, psychological problems etc.

Structure of the report

Given the questions being addressed in this study and the data available for examination, this report is structured as follows. The next chapter will use the administrative data on all pupils in the country to investigate under-achievement. In particular, the characteristics of individuals more likely to under-achieve will be identified. This is essentially a scene-setting chapter, showing who is under-achieving, and to what extent.

Chapter 3 will then switch focus to the disengagement variable, as measured by truancy. If the same type of individuals are associated with disengagement in Chapter 3 and under-achievement in Chapter 2, this would present some initial evidence of a relationship between the two.

Chapter 4 will, however, examine the relationship more directly, thus examining to what extent under-achievement is a consequence of disengagement, before continuing by examining what action can be taken by individuals who were disengaged and have under-achieved, in terms of re-engaging with learning, and if they do so, what success they have.

Chapter 5 then considers whether such re-engagement was worthwhile in terms of the labour market outcomes associated with such learning. At this point of the project, it is necessary to bring in a new data set, given that the data sets used so far (PLASC/NPD) either do not follow individuals into the labour market or they observe individuals in the labour market for only a very short period of time (YCS). Therefore the Labour Force Survey (LFS) is used for the analysis described in Chapter 5, since the primary aim of this data set is the documentation of people's working lives. The downside is that the LFS does not contain information on individuals' time at school, and so the previous indicator of disengagement (truancy) will not be available for this analysis. Indeed, the only variables available in the LFS related to time spent in school are the products of that time, namely qualifications obtained. Thus school qualifications, or more precisely the lack of good school qualifications, will be taken as an indicator of possible disengagement. Again it must be stressed that it is not being argued that disengagement was definitely the cause of individuals' lack of qualifications; it is simply being argued that a lack of school qualifications, imperfect as it is, is the best available indicator of possible previous disengagement in the national data set that also contains detailed information on respondents' labour market outcomes. Thus, given that Chapter 4 will show that low GCSE performance is a likely outcome for truants, so it is argued that the labour market outcomes for those without school qualifications will be a good indicator of the outcomes a former truant can expect.

The project considers various aspects and stages of the disengagement process, from the initial factors associated with disengagement behaviour, through the consequences of such behaviour for achievement rates, to solutions for individuals who have disengaged and consequently under-achieved, and the impact of those solutions on their final, labour market outcomes.

Disengagement from education: a brief review of the literature

Previous work on disengagement among 14–16 year olds was summarised in Steedman and Stoney (2004. A useful outcome from this review was that it classified the disengaged into three distinct groups.

■ First, there is the 'out of touch' group. Young people who comprise this group have completely dropped out of all contact with the education system before the age of 16. Although small in size, this group obviously presents a key challenge in terms of how these young people can be re-engaged. It is, however, debatable how many from this extreme drop-out group would participate in a survey such as the YCS, and so most of the analysis presented in this report probably does not refer to this group.

■ The second group is defined as 'disaffected but in touch'. As the name suggests, this group will share many of the behaviours and attitudes of the 'out of touch' group, but not to such extreme lengths. Young people in this group have managed not to lose touch completely with the education system. This group could be defined by a failure to obtain any GCSEs at Grade C or above.

■ The final group identified are the 'one to four GCSE' group, who have acquired some GCSEs at Grade C or above, but failed to reach the 'magic number' of five. Whether this is due to a limited ability, so that they have fulfilled all that could have been expected, or whether it is due to under-achievement, disaffection and lack of application, will vary from individual to individual in this group. It is this last group that has been examined in this study.

Steedman and Stoney review evidence focusing on what steps can be taken to help these three separate groups.

For the first, most disengaged group, alternative provision consisting of one-to-one contact, being treated as an adult and the availability of progression through certification seem to work best. The authors do stress, however, that unreasonable expectations should not be placed on the progress that this group can make.

The second group is the most difficult in terms of finding solutions to successfully re-engage it. They seem to respond most positively to situations in which they are taken out of school, for example FE colleges or workplace experience or training.[2] However, there is far from a perfect template for how such schemes should work, and quality of provision, and hence outcomes, can vary greatly. In addition, while it is hoped that improved motivation in the alternative setting will feed back into increased motivation for school studies, another reaction could be that these individuals merely have their ideas that school is not for them confirmed, so that attendance and motivation could actually fall. More generally, schoolwork could suffer simply as a result of being away from school. Finally, the reported improvement in motivation from attending such provision does not seem to be transferred into increased attainment in many cases. Perhaps the goal of five good GCSEs remains beyond this group at the age of 16, which suggests that alternative modes of assessment could be introduced to allow such young people to build up to a Level 2 qualification more slowly, rather than having the all-or-nothing situation of GCSEs at age 16. It should be noted that the study reported here will not be able to assess the impact of such alternative assessments on motivation, since data on such concepts as motivation is not available in the data sets being examined in this study, although the impact of qualification acquisition on future outcomes is presented later on in this report.

[2] Such ideas are reviewed further by McCrone and Morris (2004).

For the group who acquire some, but not five, good GCSEs, the proposed solution is to offer a broader range of options pre-16, in particular, vocational options, in order to improve motivation and increase the probability of young people finding areas in which they can succeed. This solution seems to be generally accepted, although there are still issues to be addressed concerning its successful implementation, such as funding being in place to cover the higher costs of providing vocational courses, and the availability of sufficient teachers with the required knowledge to teach vocational courses. Again, all that can be assessed here, however, is the impact of qualification acquisition, particularly vocational qualifications, on post-compulsory education participation and labour market outcomes.

Further studies reviewed by Steedman and Stoney (2004) show that, after the age of 16, vocational qualifications can be useful in getting previously disengaged learners, who have failed to obtain any school-level qualifications, into regular employment. Unqualified young women, in particular, seem to be most of risk of exclusion from the labour market, and so can benefit from the acquisition of vocational qualifications.

As part of the same overall project that produced the Steedman and Stoney (2004) paper,[3] a report produced by McCrone and Morris (2004) also considered disengagement by 14–16 year olds, and in particular looked at the role that vocational education can play in reducing disengagement in this group. Such education could be either studying for vocational qualifications in school or college, or undertaking work-based training via some sort of placement. Their report included a literature review of available research on this issue, as well as new evidence from interviews undertaken by the authors.

The review of the literature undertaken by McCrone and Morris revealed various benefits of vocational education for disaffected 14–16 year olds. In particular, such education seems to lead to improved motivation, both for completing current courses and continuing education beyond the age of 16, improved attendance and behaviour, increased confidence and self-esteem, and greater preparedness for post-16 education. The interviews that McCrone and Morris conducted with a group of young people, who had previously participated in vocational courses at an FE college while aged 14–16, confirmed many of these results. The interviewees explained why they liked the courses they were doing and why they enjoyed the feeling of being in college rather than in school. The reasons included, the 'greater respect' they received in college, the more individual nature of the teaching, the increased use of groupwork among students and the practical nature of courses allowing hands-on experience. These positive feelings translate into (self-reported) improved attendance and behaviour, at least while at college, although not always while back at school as well, plus an improved outlook on education and a desire to continue studies beyond the age of 16. McCrone and Morris conclude that these courses have been successful in terms of re-engaging this group of students, although their research does not allow them to say whether the success is due to the vocational nature of the courses in particular, or simply to the general fact that they are held in colleges, allowing pupils to feel 'more grown-up' and to enjoy the increased attention from teachers. The research presented here similarly cannot address such issues.

3
Skills for All project undertaken by researchers at the Centre for Economic Performance, London School of Economics and at the National Foundation for Educational Research. Details can be found on the website at http://cep.lse.ac.uk/research/skills/skillsforall.asp

Since the publication of the two reviews described above, further research has been published on the topics of disengagement or under-achievement. Such research has sought to find out which young people become disengaged and disaffected with education. Statistical data reveal that they are more likely to be:

- on the SEN register
- statemented
- on a child protection register
- receiving free school meals
- low achievers at national examinations (Schagen *et al.* 2004).

It is hoped that many of these findings will be supported by the results presented in this report. Although the quantitative findings are supported and amplified by qualitative data, it is worth highlighting aspects of the last that are only obliquely referred to, but are significant. Those who are not succeeding are usually disaffected. An obvious corollary of this statement is that those who succeed are engaged. It therefore follows that when learning, young people need to be given tasks that, although not easy, are nonetheless achievable, and that educators should help young people to think of themselves as successful and not as failures. That such disaffected young people suffer from low self-esteem (Salmon n–d) is very pertinent.

Qualitative studies have revealed other details about those who are disengaged. They tend to exhibit disruptive behaviour and may well be taking illicit drugs and/or drinking alcohol. It is common for them to have experienced domestic violence and to have had a violent parent. They could well have been victims of physical or sexual abuse within the family (Salmon n–d, Webb and Vulliamy 2004). It is also common for such young people to have a depressed parent (Webb and Vulliamy 2004). Such evidence is much more likely to emerge from case study research rather than the analysis of large data sets as presented here, showing the importance of collecting both types of evidence.

Other authors also connect disengagement with family circumstances. Dalziel and Henthorne (2005) find that young people who are playing truant from school are likely to come from families trying to cope with a series of major difficulties, such as debt, poor health and housing. Philip *et al.* (2004, p4) relate disengagement with 'the influence of poverty, early child difficulties and inequalities in health'. Broadhurst *et al.* (2005, p109) also find that disengaged young people come from families that 'were disadvantaged along a number of dimensions, including lone parenting, poor housing, dependency on state benefits and a history of domestic violence and mental health problems'. Family background will be a key component of this study.

The study by Webb *et al.* (2004) emphasises that family problems lead in turn to disruptive behaviour that then leads to lack of achievement and hence to disengagement. Although its sample is not representative, it is perhaps pertinent that three-quarters of the young people in the study did not live with two parents.

The Webb study also draws attention to how the disengaged can be those who feel alienated by the culture of school. For example, there may be frequent clashes over grooming and school uniform. A pupil who had just been a victim of abuse found that the only thing the school was interested in was that he was wearing trainers, instead of the regulation shoes. However, both this study and one by Morrison (2004) show how a positive school culture combined with effective support can promote engagement and help vulnerable young people to overcome difficulties.

Similarly, Attwood *et al.* (2004a, 2004b) have undertaken a case study of a programme whereby an FE college took disaffected Year 10 and 11 students from local schools. Twenty-six per cent had been excluded, 30% were persistent non-attenders and the rest were failing to achieve in their lessons at school. At the FE college they were put on vocational courses, such as motor mechanics and hairdressing. The first report (2004a) contains an important finding that *these students were not negative about education per se: they were negative about schooling.* The second report (2004b) provides some reasons for this. Although about a third of the students had stated they did not like the school curriculum, they overwhelmingly complained about their relationships with teachers. They felt picked on and, in particular, not respected. Underpinning all this, there seemed to have been a dislike of the school culture.

At the FE college, by contrast, they liked the different culture, the way tutors were helpful and caring and they felt they were treated with respect. However, it is also relevant that they were motivated by the vocational curriculum, because they could understand its purpose. All the same, another important finding was that they tended to have serious social problems at home and did not feel themselves to be in control of their own destiny; they felt their lives were out of their control.

All the above researchers imply or overtly support the view of Salmon (n–d) that emotional problems can get in the way of learning and often need to be tackled before these young people are able to learn. However, this still leaves unanswered the question why some from disadvantaged backgrounds with emotional problems are nevertheless able to engage with learning. It is likely that any socio-cultural explanation needs to be balanced with an understanding of the individual, inherent characteristics, to acquire a complete picture.

2 Individual characteristics associated with under-achievement in Key stage test results

Introduction

The aim of this chapter is to describe rates of under-achievement and the characteristics of individuals who under-achieve, given that under-achievement and low school exam results are a big part of the disengagement story that follows.

Under-achievement is being defined here in terms of individuals' Key stage test results. These tests are taken at ages 7, 11, 14 and 16 (Key stages 1–4 respectively), and data sets are available that record scores in these tests – the National Pupil Database (NPD), and which can also be matched to the Pupil Level Annual School Census (PLASC), containing information on the characteristics of each pupil. Note that the NPD/PLASC data set is not just a representative sample, but is actually the full population of pupils in each year group. Observation numbers are therefore extremely large for this analysis. The next section describes this data set, and the methodology to be pursued in this chapter.

The NPD/PLASC data set, and the measurement of under-achievement

4
With the maths and science tests, the situation is complicated by the fact that there are different 'tiers' of the tests that pupils can take, which vary in complexity. The level to which pupils are allocated reflects the tier to which they were allocated. Thus for example, a test score of 50 could imply achievement at Level 3 on a lower tier test, but achievement at Level 4 on a higher tier test. All of this was allowed for when allocating pupils to levels based on their test scores.

The NPD/PLASC data set is a valuable resource – made available only recently – in that it contains the whole population of pupils in state schools, and contains the information required to link background characteristics of individuals to their exam performance. This is not just their performance in end-of-school exams such as GCSEs, but also results of all Key stage tests. This study does not consider Key stage 1, because the data has not been collected over a time period long enough to ensure that the 16 year olds in the most recent data set available (2003) were also recorded at Key stage 1 nine years previously. However, data from 1998 is available, and so the group who reached Key stage 4 in 2003 are observed at Key stage 2 in 1998. We also have data on their Key stage 3 results in 2001.

At Key stages 2 and 3, individuals take tests in English, maths and science. On the basis of their test scores they are allocated to a level of achievement, which can go up to Level 5 at Key stage 2 and Level 6 at Key stage 3.[4] To give overall achievement at Key stages 2 and 3, the levels reached for each of the English, maths and science tests were simply summed, giving a maximum 'score' of 15 at Key stage 2 and 18 at Key stage 3. Key stage 4 is the end of compulsory schooling, when pupils take their GCSEs. Achievement at Key stage 4 was therefore measured by pupils' total GCSE point score, with eight points scored for an A*, seven points for an A, six points for a B etc.

It is of interest, given the following analysis – which defines under-achievement in terms of performance at one Key stage relative to performance at an earlier Key stage – to look at performance figures on the tests taken at these Key stages, and to illustrate how people's performance can change at different Key stages. In Table 2.1, performance at each Key stage is defined to be above, at or below the average of all individuals at that Key stage. The cut-off point for below-average performance is one standard deviation (SD) below the average score on the test in question, and similarly the cut-off point for above-average performance is one standard deviation above the mean. Average performance is then defined to be between these standard deviations around the mean. If the test scores are normally distributed, this means that about 16% of the population will be defined as above and below average at each Key stage, which is a bit arbitrary and mechanical. Of most interest therefore is the number of pupils who change their performance levels across Key stages. In each of the cells in Table 2.1, the number of pupils falling within the cell is shown, and then this is expressed as a percentage of the 444,234 individuals with usable data in the data set.

The results show that, as expected, by far the most dense cell is the one in the centre, containing just over half of the pupil population, who are the ones with average performance at each of the three Key stages considered. The number in the bottom right-hand corner of the table shows that 8.5% of the population achieve above-average performance, on the definitions used here, throughout their school careers at all three Key stages considered. In the top left-hand corner, on the other hand, only 2.8% of the population are classified as having below-average performance at each Key stage. Thus more pupils move out of the below-average group than fall out of the above-average group.

5
Of course, the use of the relative, standard deviation measure means that some people will almost certainly be defined as under-achieving for any usual distribution of actual scores, no matter how well the population has done in absolute terms. For example, if the distribution of GCSE scores follows a standard normal distribution, then 16% of the population will have a score one standard deviation below the mean. The one standard deviation measure has been used in other literatures, however, such as the over-/under-education literature. In such research, the required level of education for a particular job or occupation is taken to be the average education level (years of education) in that occupation, while anyone with one standard deviation more (less) education is defined as over-/under-educated.

Table 2.1
Distribution of pupils by performance at the three Key stages
Data source: Pupil Level Annual School Census/National Pupil Database
SD = Standard deviation

	Performance at Key stage 4		
	> 1 SD below the average	Within 1 SD of the average	> 1 SD above the average
Performance at Key stage 3 > 1 SD below the average			
Key stage 2 < average	12,254 (2.8%)	14,901 (3.4%)	27 (0.0%)
Key stage 2 average	8,717 (2.0%)	12,686 (2.9%)	28 (0.0%)
Key stage 2 > average	29 (0.0%)	46 (0.0%)	0 (0.0%)
Performance at Key stage 3 within 1 SD of the average			
Key stage 2 < average	2,682 (0.6%)	19,206 (4.3%)	275 (0.0%)
Key stage 2 average	15,886 (3.6%)	225,194 (50.7%)	17,739 (4.0%)
Key stage 2 > average	530 (0.1%)	15,286 (3.4%)	3,177 (0.7%)
Performance at Key stage 3 > 1 SD above the average			
Key stage 2 < average	3 (0.0%)	13 (0.0%)	27 (0.0%)
Key stage 2 average	177 (0.0%)	19,757 (4.4%)	19,283 (4.3%)
Key stage 2 > average	246 (0.1%)	18,112 (4.1%)	37,953 (8.5%)

6
Note that this definition uses a lot more information than that used to construct Table 2.1, since the average Key stage 4 points score, against which each individual's relative performance is calculated, is derived separately for every single level of Key stage 3 performance, rather than just looking at the deviations from the single mean score across all individuals at Key stage 4.

7
A recent publication by the Office of National Statistics (ONS) and the DfES (DfES 2005) looks at the characteristics of low-attaining pupils, and defines low attainment in an absolute and relative way. Absolute low attainment is defined to scoring lower than the 'expected' level at each Key stage (for example, pupils are expected to reach Level 4 at Key stage 2), while the relative measure considers those in the lowest quartile (ie the lowest 25%) of attainment at a Key stage. Thus no consideration is given to the pupils' performance on earlier Key stage tests, and this is why the measures are said to be of low attainment, rather than of under-achievement as defined here. The characteristics they find to be associated with low attainment, however, are similar to those found here to be related to under-achievement.

This is an important theme that will be picked up at various points: that low achievement is not permanent and pupils can get their learning back on track.

The characteristics of those pupils who successfully learn again are examined later on in this chapter. In terms of the numbers involved, 3.4% of the population are below average at both Key stages 2 and 3, but nevertheless get average (as defined here) GCSE (ie Key stage 4) results, while 4.3% of the population are below average at Key stage 2, but get up to average by Key stage 3 and stay there in Key stage 4. It also has to be said that there is negligible movement from below average to above average across Key stages.

For the purposes of this report, under-achievement could have been defined by identifying individuals whose performance slipped down from, for example, above average to average or from average to below average. It is, however, possible to use a more sophisticated measure of under-achievement, given these Key stage test scores. Since the scores at each Key stage are measured on different scales, comparing the actual numbers themselves would not be appropriate.

The method chosen can be illustrated using under-achievement at Key stage 4 on the basis of Key stage 3 test results as an example. For each possible level of achievement at Key stage 3, from a minimum of 3 points to a maximum of 18, the average GCSE points score at Key stage 4 was calculated. Anyone scoring more than one standard deviation below this average was then defined as under-achieving. The use of the standard deviation measure rather than some absolute amount gets around the problem of different scales being used at each Key stage.[5] For example, if, among those with a score of 10 at Key stage 3, the average GCSE points score is 40 with standard deviation of 10, then anyone scoring 10 at Key stage 3 and then less than 30 at Key stage 4 is defined to be under-achieving.[6] Such under-achievement indicators were derived for Key stage 4 (GCSE) outcomes on the basis of Key stage 3 results, Key stage 4 outcomes on the basis of Key stage 2 results and Key stage 3 outcomes on the basis of Key stage 2 results.[7]

Thus a very particular measure of under-achievement is used. It should be noted that individuals characterised here as under-achievers need not necessarily have achieved poor GCSE results, for example, but only results not as good as they could have obtained, based on the evidence provided by their earlier test scores. Thus someone who scored at the top level of 18 at Key stage 3, but at Key stage 4 only managed to obtain six GCSEs could end up being defined as an under-achiever using the current methodology, even though in absolute terms they would usually be thought of as a success. An alternative is to use the absolute measure, and define under-achievers as anyone who obtains fewer than five good GCSEs. On this basis, however, the person with few natural abilities, who works very hard and puts in maximum effort to obtain four good GCSEs would be defined as under-achieving. At various points in the chapter, we will therefore combine the relative and the absolute measures, and define an under-achiever at Key stage 4 to be an individual who scores one standard deviation below the average Key stage 4 test score for individuals with the same Key stage 3 test results *and* who also fails to achieve five or more good GCSEs (or simply five or more GCSEs whatever their grade).

Given these new measures adopted, the results show that at Key stage 3, 17% of the population of 14 year olds in 2001 under-achieved compared to their Key stage 2 test results. Similarly, at Key stage 4 (GCSE), 13% of the same population in 2003, now aged 16, under-achieved compared to their Key stage 3 test results. However, there appear to be two distinct stages of under-achievement, and the people who under-achieve at Key stage 3 are far from being the same people who under-achieve again at Key stage 4. Thus, of those who under-achieve at Key stage 3, most (83%) do not fall behind even further by doing worse at Key stage 4 than their, already lower, Key stage 3 results would have predicted. Similarly, of those who under-achieve in their GCSEs compared to what their Key stage 3 results predicted they should have done, most (78%) had not under-achieved at Key stage 3. Thus there seems to be one group of individuals who fall behind after Key stage 2 (age 11), while another group do not start to fall behind until after Key stage 3 (age 14). The statistical analyses that follow will shed some light on the characteristics of these two groups.

One possibility we have not considered yet is where pupils under-achieve at Key stage 3 compared to what their Key stage 2 results would have predicted, but nevertheless get the GCSE results that their Key stage 2 results predicted (and not the results that their lower Key Stage 3 results, as in the previous paragraph, predicted). Such a group would therefore be falling behind between the ages of 11 and 14, but between the ages of 14 and 16 get themselves sorted out and back on track, and achieve the GCSE results that their age 11 performance always predicted they would. Again, the final analysis in this chapter will reveal the characteristics of the pupils who turn their performance around in this way. The data suggests that such individuals are quite a large group; of those who under-achieve at Key stage 3 relative to their Key stage 2 results, 62% nevertheless get the GCSE results that their Key stage 2 results predicted that they should have done. Obviously, the remaining 38% do not get back on track and so under-achieve at both Key stages 3 and 4, relative to their Key stage 2 predictions. Similarly, of those who under-achieve in their GCSEs, relative to what their Key stage 2 scores predicted, just over half (53%) had already under-achieved by Key stage 3, which of course means that the other half under-achieve for the first time between the ages of 14 and 16.

Raw data for under-achievement variables, and the cross-tabulation with individual characteristics

Before the statistical analysis, we present some raw data in table and graph form. Table 2.2 and Figure 2.1 display the results for the rate of under-achievement at Key stage 3, on the basis of Key stage 2 test results.

Figure 2.1 shows that boys have a higher rate of under-achievement at Key stage 3 compared to girls, but the difference is very small. Much larger differences exist across ethnic groups. The highest rates of under-achievement at Key stage 3 are observed for Afro-Caribbean black pupils (30%), other black pupils (29%), African black and Bangladeshi (both 23%) pupils.[8] In contrast, the rate of under-achievement at Key stage 3 among Chinese pupils is five times lower than the Afro-Caribbean rate (ie 6%), with the next lowest rate being 12%, among Indian pupils.

The final bars in Figure 2.1 reveal the results that pupils who receive free school meals (as an indicator of social background) are much more likely to under-achieve at Key stage 3 than those with no such entitlement (28% versus 16%), while pupils with SEN[9] are more likely to under-achieve than pupils without such special needs. The under-achievement rate is actually higher among non-statemented than among statemented SEN pupils, although the difference is not large. One interpretation of this result is that it proves the success of statementing, in that it reduces under-achievement. It is possible, however, that those pupils who receive a statement of SEN are those with the most easily defined needs, while those without a statement may have more complex needs, which could explain their higher rate of under-achievement.

8
The huge number of observations in the PLASC/NPD data set allows much more disaggregated division of ethnic groups than the YCS data used in Chapters 3 and 4.

9
It would have been useful to include indicators of the type of special educational need (SEN), since these can differ widely from serious difficulties to hearing problems. Unfortunately, such an indicator was not available in the 2003 data set, and was due to be added to PLASC in 2004.

Table 2.2
Rates of under-achievement at Key stage 3 relative to Key stage 2
Data source: Pupil Level Annual School Census/National Pupil Database

Male	17.3
Female	16.5
White British	16.6
Other white	16.8
Mixed race	19.0
Indian	12.1
Pakistani	20.1
Bangladeshi	23.4
Chinese	6.3
Other Asian	12.4
Afro-Caribbean black	29.5
African black	23.1
Other black	28.9
Other	16.2
Entitled to free school meals	27.6
Not entitled to free school meals	15.6
SEN pupils with statement	29.1
SEN pupils without statement	32.4
No SEN	15.5

Figure 2.1
Rates of under-achievement at Key stage 3 relative to Key stage 2
Data source: Pupil Level Annual School Census/National Pupil Database

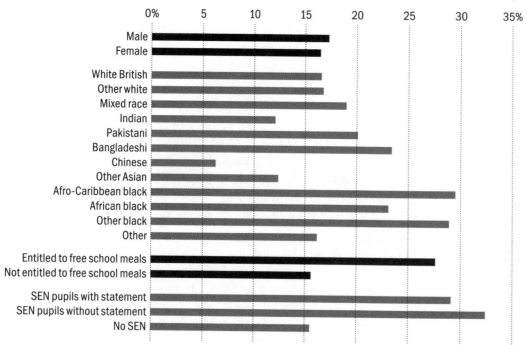

Table 2.3 and Figure 2.2 present the results of a similar analysis for under-achievement rates at Key stage 4 (GCSE), relative to scores predicted on the basis of Key stage 3 results. Figure 2.2 reveals some interesting differences compared to Figure 2.1, suggesting that it is somewhat different groups who under-achieve between the ages of 14 and 16, compared to under-achievers between the ages of 11 and 14. In particular, the gender results reveal a definite difference now, 16% of boys but just 10% of girls under-achieving in their GCSEs. The ethnic group results display some key changes. The highest rate of under-achievement at Key stage 4 relative to Key stage 3 is still among 'other black' pupils although the size of the effect (15%) is much smaller than the size of the effects observed at Key stage 3. The next highest rates of Key stage 4 under-achievement are for mixed-race (14%) and white British pupils (13%). These results suggest that much of the under-achievement among black pupils surfaces between the ages of 11 and 14, beyond which their chances of further deterioration are merely average. White British pupils, however, seem to be relatively more susceptible to under-achieve between the ages of 14 and 16.

The discussion of the raw figures has helped to illuminate characteristics of the groups who begin under-achieving between the ages of 11 and 14, and between the ages of 14 and 16. The results presented here suggest that the former group are more likely to contain black pupils, while the latter group are relatively more likely to be white British males. Chinese pupils also seem to do relatively worse between Key stages 3 and 4, compared to the earlier period between Key stages 2 and 3. In the earlier period, they had the lowest under-achievement rate, while in the latter period, their under-achievement rate of 7% is higher than that of Indians (5%), Pakistanis, Bangladeshis and African black pupils (all 6%) – though it is worth noting that under-achievement for the Chinese group is being measured relative to a higher starting point, given its good Key stage 3 results.

Table 2.3
Rates of under-achievement at Key stage 4 relative to Key stage 3
Data source: Pupil Level Annual School Census/National Pupil Database

Male	16.0
Female	9.7
White British	13.2
Other white	10.7
Mixed race	14.2
Indian	4.6
Pakistani	5.7
Bangladeshi	6.3
Chinese	7.1
Other Asian	6.1
Afro-Caribbean black	12.9
African black	6.2
Other black	15.3
Other	10.7
Entitled to free school meals	20.4
Not entitled to free school meals	11.7
SEN pupils with statement	23.7
SEN pupils without statement	26.1
No SEN	11.3

Figure 2.2
Rates of under-achievement at Key stage 4 relative to Key stage 3
Data source: Pupil Level Annual School Census/National Pupil Database

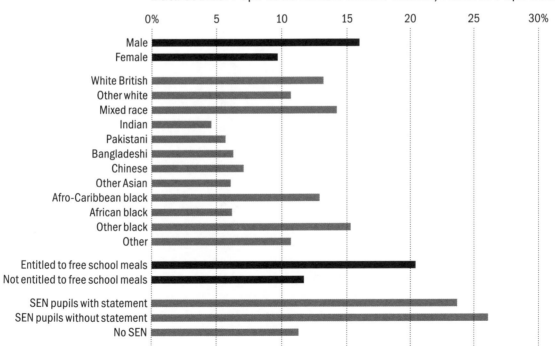

As mentioned in the previous section, an alternative indicator of under-achievement at Key stage 4 considers those who score more than one standard deviation below the average Key stage 4 mark of all those who obtained the same Key stage 3 score, as above, but who also fail to obtain five or more good GCSEs. This removes the possibility of someone with, for example, seven good GCSEs being defined as an under-achiever because they were predicted to obtain nine good GCSEs. The under-achievement rates according to this new definition are presented for the various individual characteristics in Table 2.4 and Figure 2.3. This figure would be expected to differ significantly from Figure 2.2 only if individuals with certain characteristics are particularly likely to be characterised by the example just given, whereby they under-achieve relative to what they were predicted to obtain at GCSE, but nevertheless still obtain five or more good GCSEs.

Figure 2.3 and Table 2.4 reveal that there is not a change in the pattern of results when individuals with five or more good GCSEs are stripped out of the group defined as under-achieving at Key stage 4. All of the bars in Figure 2.3 fall by around 2 percentage points relative to Figure 2.2, and none fall by more than 3 percentage points. It therefore seems that no one demographic group's under-achievers at Key stage 4 are dominated by individuals who nevertheless secure at least five good GCSEs. Therefore relative under-achievement rates across demographic groups will not be affected by the inclusion or exclusion of those with five or more good GCSEs.

Table 2.4
**Rates of under-achievement at Key stage 4 relative to Key stage 3
at the same time failing to obtain five good GCSEs**
Data source: Pupil Level Annual School Census/National Pupil Database

Male	12.4
Female	7.7
White British	10.3
Other white	8.6
Mixed race	11.3
Indian	2.8
Pakistani	4.7
Bangladeshi	5.2
Chinese	4.3
Other Asian	4.5
Afro-Caribbean black	11.4
African black	5.1
Other black	13.7
Other	8.6
Entitled to free school meals	18.7
Not entitled to free school meals	8.8
SEN pupils with statement	22.5
SEN pupils without statement	24.9
No SEN	8.4

Figure 2.3
**Rates of under-achievement at Key stage 4 relative to Key stage 3
at the same time failing to obtain five good GCSEs**
Data source: Pupil Level Annual School Census/National Pupil Database

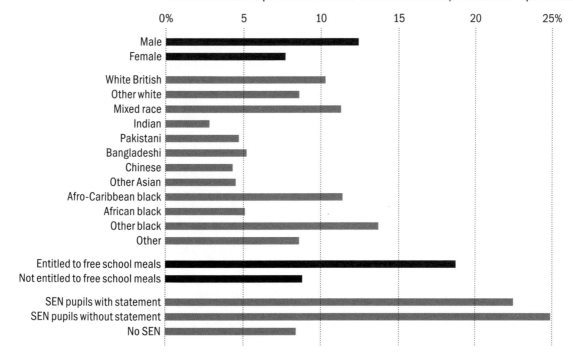

Finally in this section we look at those who under-achieve and fail to obtain five GCSEs at *any* grade at Key stage 4, rather than five GCSEs at Grade C or above. Failing to acquire five GCSEs at any grade (even a G) is a more stringent indicator of disengagement, and suggests that individuals really have made little attempt to learn, or perhaps did not even enter the examination in some or all of their GCSE subjects. As such, failure to reach this lower benchmark is perhaps less likely to be influenced by factors such as natural ability, and more likely to be identifying real disengagement. The downside of using this definition is that it does not capture many individuals, but only perhaps a hardcore of disengaged pupils, and for this reason it will only ever be used to complement the five or more GCSEs at Grades A*–C measure, rather than substitute for it. Thus, in the data set used here, only 11% of the pupils fail to acquire at least five Grade A*–G GCSEs, and only 3.8% of the population are picked up when we look at those who under-achieve *and* fail to get five GCSEs of any grade.[10] Table 2.5 and Figure 2.4 reveal the rates of such low performance *and* under-achievement by pupil characteristics.

10
These two facts imply that many of those who fail to get five GCSEs at any grade do not under-achieve according to the relative measure used here, and thus must have struggled throughout their school careers.

Table 2.5
Rates of under-achievement at Key stage 4 relative to Key stage 3
at the same time failing to obtain five GCSEs at any grade
Data source: Pupil Level Annual School Census/National Pupil Database

Male	4.2
Female	3.4
White British	3.9
Other white	3.8
Mixed race	4.7
Indian	0.9
Pakistani	1.9
Bangladeshi	2.0
Chinese	1.8
Other Asian	1.8
Afro-Caribbean black	4.5
African black	2.0
Other black	6.6
Other	3.7
Entitled to free school meals	8.2
Not entitled to free school meals	3.1
SEN pupils with statement	9.2
SEN pupils without statement	11.5
No SEN	2.8

Figure 2.4
Rates of under-achievement at Key stage 4 relative to Key stage 3
at the same time failing to obtain five GCSEs at any grade
Data source: Pupil Level Annual School Census/National Pupil Database

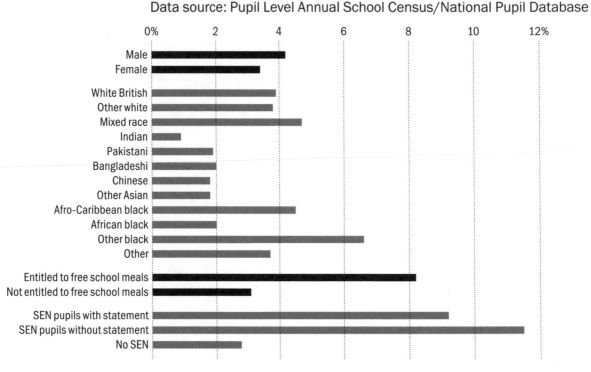

These results reveal that when attention is focused on this small group who under-achieve relative to earlier performance and fail to get five GCSEs at Grade G or above, the same characteristics emerge again as correlates. Thus boys, white, Afro-Caribbean and 'other black' pupil groups, those entitled to free school meals and those with SEN, emerge as being more likely to under-achieve and have low performance, according to this definition. This implies that the choice of the five or more GCSE at Grades A*–C indicator does not significantly affect the results, and we can have faith in using this measure throughout this study.

Key points

This section identified the characteristics of individuals associated with the likelihood of under-achieving in the raw data, thus not controlling for any other characteristics. At Key stage 3, under-achievement on the basis of Key stage 2 results is most common among:

- boys
- Afro-Caribbean black, African black, other black and Bangladeshi pupils
- those entitled to free school meals
- those with special educational needs.

At Key stage 4, under-achievement on the basis of Key stage 3 results is most common among:

- boys (with the gender difference getting larger than at Key stage 3)
- other black, mixed-race, and white British pupils
- those entitled to free school meals
- those with special educational needs.

There is therefore some evidence that if black pupils under-achieve, the process begins between the ages of 11 and 14 (Key stages 2 and 3), whereas for white pupils, and particularly white boys who under-achieve, the decline is more likely to set in between the ages of 14 and 16 (Key stages 3 and 4).

The factors associated with under-achievement: multivariate analysis[11]

As will be the case throughout this report, the presentation of the raw data is followed by a multivariate analysis of the data, which reveals the true effect of each variable on under-achievement, holding the effects of all other included variables constant.

Under-achievement at Key stage 3 on the basis of Key stage 2 results

Table A2.1 in the Regression Appendix at the end of this chapter looks first at the determinants of under-achievement at Key Stage 3, on the basis of Key stage 2 results. Since the dependent variable is a dummy variable,[12] taking the value of 1 or 0 to indicate the presence or absence of under-achievement, the estimation method must be chosen to reflect the fact that the dependent variable has this property and is not a linear variable. The correct method to use is a probit equation.[13] The coefficients reported in Table A2.1 are actually marginal effects derived from the estimated coefficients, and therefore indicate in each case the difference in the probability of under-achieving between individuals with the characteristic defined by the particular dummy variable in question and individuals with the characteristic defined by the omitted category.

Looking in the first column of results, we can see that, holding other factors constant, girls are less likely to under-achieve at Key stage 3 than boys, but only by 0.2 percentage points. This difference is nevertheless statistically significant, aided by the huge number of observations.

The coefficients on the ethnic group variables reveal the under-achievement rate for each group, relative to the omitted group,[14] which is white British pupils. The ordering of the ethnic groups with respect to the Key stage 3 under-achievement rate is the same as in the raw data, with the highest rate found among Afro-Caribbean black pupils and the lowest rate among Chinese pupils. The size of some of the effects is much lower than those the raw data – with its large differences in under-achievement rates as pictured in Figure 2.1 – might have predicted, however. For example, the results in column one suggest that African black pupils have an under-achievement rate at Key stage 3 only 2.7 percentage points above that of white British pupils. This reveals the importance of holding constant social background, via the free school meals variable in this analysis, when comparing outcomes across ethnic groups.

The final results in column one confirm that pupils who receive free school meals, and pupils with SEN are significantly more likely to under-achieve at Key stage 3.

11
The analysis presented so far has looked at the relationship between under-achievement and each characteristic in turn of individuals, in isolation from the other characteristics. Multivariate regression analysis looks at the relationship between a dependent variable, in this case under-achievement, and a list of explanatory variables (in this case, gender, ethnicity, free school meal and SEN status) together, thus examining how much of the variation in under-achievement is explained by the group of explanatory variables as a whole. The big advantage of using a multivariate technique such as regression analysis, rather than simply looking at the relationship between under-achievement and each variable on its own is that regression analysis allows the researcher to observe the 'pure' effect of each explanatory variable in turn, holding constant in each case the effects of all other variables in the estimated equation.

12
Many variables are not quantitative, but nevertheless are still important variables that researchers wish to include in their regression analyses. For example, while under-achievement could have been measured numerically, by the number of grades an individual was below their expected level, it was actually measured here qualitatively; individuals either under-achieved or they did not. Other variables in the analysis can always only be measured qualitatively, for example gender; either the individual respondent is female or not. There is no number that can be attached to 'femaleness'. Since regression analysis requires numerical data, dummy variables allow researchers to include such qualitative characteristics in their equations. ▶ Continued

12 ▶ Continued
They always take the value
of 1 or 0 for all observations.
For example, the 'female'
dummy variable takes
the value of 1 for female
respondents and 0
for male respondents.

13
The probit estimator
is a maximum likelihood
estimator. The coefficients
are therefore chosen by
the estimation procedure
to maximise the probability,
or likelihood, that the predicted
under-achievement status
given these coefficients
matches the actual
under-achievement status.

14
When dummy variables
are included in an equation,
one possible variation of
the characteristic in question
is always excluded from
the equation, to form the
reference category or omitted
group. The coefficients on
the included dummy variables
then measure the difference
in the dependent variable
between individuals with
the included characteristic(s)
and individuals with the
excluded characteristic.
For example, with respect
to gender, this can obviously
only be one of two possibilities
in each observation. Thus one
dummy variable is included,
'female' being chosen as the
included group in this report,
with the coefficient on the
female dummy variable
then indicating the extent of
under-achievement among
females relative to the
omitted group, males. With
respect to ethnicity, there are
12 ethnic groups defined in
the data, and so 11 dummy
variables were included in
the estimated equations.
The reference category or
omitted group was chosen
to be 'white British pupils',
and so the difference in
under-achievement between
white British pupils and
all other ethnic groups is
indicated by the coefficients on
the included dummy variables.

A possibility that should be explored is that the ethnic group effects could differ according to other characteristics. Given the data set on the whole population being used in this analysis, it is possible to examine the interaction of ethnicity variables with the gender, SEN status and free school meals variables.[15] The results from this analysis are presented in column two of Table A2.1. The interpretation of the coefficients on the standard ethnicity dummy variables is now the difference in Key stage 3 under-achievement rates between white British pupils, boys with no SEN and no entitlement to free school meals, and similarly defined boys in the ethnic group in question. The coefficients on the interaction terms tell us whether the impact of belonging to that ethnic grouping differs across genders, SEN status or free school meal entitlement.

Looking at the results in column two, the effects for boys only show the same ranking of under-achievement rates as for the full population in column one. Looking at the interaction terms, there are statistically significant differences in the effect of belonging to an ethnic group between boys and girls for 'other white pupils' and Afro-Caribbean black pupils. The coefficient on the latter variable, for example, reveals that the higher under-achievement rate at Key stage 3 among Afro-Caribbean pupils is not as bad – 2 percentage points less – for girls in that group as it is for boys in that group.

Of perhaps most interest is the fact that a number of the coefficients on the interaction terms between ethnic origin and the receipt of free school meals are negative and statistically significant (specifically on the Indian, Pakistani, Bangladeshi, Afro-Caribbean black, African black and other black group interaction). These results suggest that the positive association between free school meal entitlement and under-achievement (an 11.5 percentage point higher under-achievement rate among white pupils receiving free school meals relative to those not on free school meals) is not as strong for these ethnic groups, ie the under-achievement gap across the free school meals/no free school meals group rate among these ethnic groups is 3–5 percentage points lower than the 11.5 figure for white pupils.

Thus poverty (assuming free school meal eligibility is an indicator of poverty) is less of a reason for under-achievement, specifically among pupils from the Indian sub-continent and the African ethnic groups compared to white pupils; or, to put it another way, proportionally more individuals in the former groups born into poverty manage to avoid under-achieving, compared to white pupils.[16]

15
The number of observations
in each cell is given in the
final column of Table A2.1.
It is true that the number
of observations in the
SEN with statement –
ethnic background cells
are very small relative to
the size of the data set,
and indeed only one of
them achieves a statistically
significant coefficient.
For all other cells, however,
the number of observations
should be sufficient.

16
Note that another possibility
that has been suggested is
that free school meals may
be a less reliable indicator
of social background among
ethnic minority groups, if the
rate of self-employment is
higher among such groups
than among white pupils.
Entitlement to free school
meals is easier to assess
among employees than among
self-employed workers.

Key points

Looking at under-achievement at Key stage 3 relative to test scores at Key Stage 2 the following results emerge:

■ The highest rate of under-achievement is among Afro-Caribbean black pupils. However, the gap with respect to the omitted category, white pupils, is smaller than in the raw data, which suggests that some of the apparent poor performance of this group represents a failure to control for social background, which appears to be influencing under-achievement.

■ Girls are slightly less likely to under-achieve than boys.

■ The negative impact of free school meal entitlement on Key stage 3 performance is lessened in the Indian, Pakistani, Bangladeshi, Afro-Caribbean black, African black and other black groups.

Under-achievement at Key stage 4 on the basis of Key stage 3 results

Table A2.2 repeats this analysis for the rate of under-achievement at Key stage 4, on the basis of Key stage 3 results. Thus for those who did not under-achieve at Key stage 3, we are asking if they start to under-achieve between the ages of 14 and 16, while for those who did under-achieve at Key stage 3, we are asking whether they manage to obtain GCSE results consistent with this lower score at Key stage 3, or whether they deteriorate further and fail to obtain the GCSEs predicted by even their lower Key stage 3 score.

The results show that, as in the raw data, the difference between girls and boys grows leading up to Key stage 4, compared to leading up to Key stage 3. Thus, boys are 6 percentage points more likely to under-achieve at GCSE than girls. The ethnic group variables almost all attract negative coefficients, most of which are statistically significant, suggesting that white British pupils are the most likely to under-achieve at Key stage 4, together with Afro-Caribbean black and other black pupils. The least likely to under-achieve, relative to their Key stage 3 results, are Indian, Pakistani and Bangladeshi pupils, who are all about 8 percentage points less likely to under-achieve at GCSE than white British pupils. Furthermore, the interaction effects in column two attract negative and statistically significant coefficients for each of these groups (of 2–3 percentage points), suggesting that the difference in GCSE under-achievement between these three ethnic groups and the white British pupils group is even larger among girls than it is among boys.

The other variables in Table A2.2, indicating receipt of free school meals and the presence of SEN, are both strongly related to more under-achievement at Key stage 4, just as they were at Key stage 3.

However, the coefficient on *every single* interaction term between the free school meal indicator and the ethnic dummy variables is negative and statistically significant, suggesting that the impact of free school meal receipt is particularly large for the omitted category, namely white pupils. For many groups (Indian, Pakistani, Bangladeshi, Chinese, Afro-Caribbean black, African black and 'other' pupils) the impact of free school meal receipt upon performance is less than half of the impact for white pupils. The performance of these groups therefore does not seem to be as affected by social deprivation as white pupils.

Table A2.3 defines under-achievers as only those who have under-achieved at Key stage 4 on the basis of their Key stage 3 results, and who have failed to acquire at least five good GCSEs. As was found in the raw data, making this change to the definition of under-achievement barely affects the pattern of results. The one difference is that the coefficients for Afro-Caribbean and other black pupils are now positive and statistically significant, suggesting a higher rate of under-achievement than white pupils, whereas in Table A2.2 they were equal. The reason is that more white pupils than black pupils are removed from the ranks of the under-achievers when those with at least five good GCSEs are stripped out of the under-achievement group, therefore leaving more black pupils among the remaining pool of under-achievers.

Table A2.4 strips out all those who obtained five GCSEs at any grade, and considers only those who under-achieve at Key stage 4 relative to Key stage 3 and fail to acquire five GCSEs even at Grade G. The results show that it is boys and white pupils (and not those in black groups in this case) who are more likely to under-achieve according to the definition. The size of the effects are smaller than before, however, since fewer individuals fall into this definition of under-achievement.

Key points

Looking at under-achievement at Key stage 4 on the basis of Key stage 3 test results, it emerges that:

■ Under-achievement is greater among boys than girls, with the gap being wider than it was at Key stage 3.

■ The white British, Afro-Caribbean black and other black ethnic groups now have the highest rate of under-achievement of all ethnic groups, while the Indian, Pakistani, Bangladeshi and other Asian groups have the lowest rate, particularly among girls in the first three cases. When attention is focused on those under-achievers who fail to obtain five GCSEs at any grade, it is white pupils who are most likely to fall into this category.

■ Under-achievement is on average higher among individuals entitled to free school meals. This is particularly so for white pupils, with the performance of other ethnic groups being much less affected by social deprivation.

Under-achievement at Key stage 4 on the basis of Key stage 2 results

Finally, what has been considered so far is whether those who under-achieved at Key stage 3 then under-achieve even further at Key stage 4 or not. What has not yet been considered in a multivariate setting, though, is whether individuals who under-achieve at Key stage 3 manage to pull themselves around and reduce or eradicate their under-achievement by Key stage 4.

The next step is to identify who, among the group who under-achieved at Key stage 3, nevertheless manage to get the GCSEs that their Key stage 2 results at age 11 always predicted they would. Table A2.5 presents just such results, looking at the determinants of under-achievement at Key stage 4 on the basis of Key stage 2 results, for the sub-sample of the population who under-achieved at Key stage 3. A negative coefficient suggests that a group was less likely to under-achieve at Key stage 4, despite having under-achieved at Key stage 3, and therefore indicates the groups who manage to turn their performance around by Key stage 4.

Looking at the results in column one, it is girls and most of the ethnic minority groups who manage to do this, relative to boys and white British pupils. The least likely to under-achieve at Key stage 4, relative to their Key stage 2 results (ie the most likely to turn their performance around) are Indian (20 percentage points less likely to under-achieve at Key stage 4 than white British pupils in this sub-sample), Pakistani and Bangladeshi (both 23 percentage points less likely) and Chinese (23 percentage points less likely) groups, with the coefficient for African black pupils also being large (18 percentage points less likely to under-achieve).

The further statistically significant coefficients in column two reveal that is it in fact girls in these ethnic groups just mentioned who seem most able to turn their performance around after under-achieving at Key stage 3. In addition, we again observe that being from a socially deprived background (entitled to free school meals) does not seem to hold back many ethnic groups as it does white British pupils, when it comes to getting their studies back on track and avoiding under-achievement at Key stage 4.

Finally, Table A2.6 shows that stripping out those who have achieved at least five *good* GCSEs from the Key stage 4 under-achievers defined above barely affects the pattern of result, as was found earlier. Table A2.7 considers only those who under-achieve at Key stage 4 on the basis of Key stage 2 results *and* fail to acquire five GCSEs at Grades A*–G (who form only 5.5% of the population) and again finds that it is white boys who are most likely to under-achieve (least likely to get their education back on track) according to this definition.

Key points

Looking for under-achievement at Key stage 4 relative to performance at Key stage 2, only for those who under-achieved at Key stage 3, allows us to investigate which of the groups under-achieving at age 14 get their studies back on track by managing to get the Key stage 4 results that their Key stage 2 marks predicted. The results suggest that the most likely to get back on track are:

■ girls

■ most of the Asian ethnic background groups, and in particular girls in these groups.

Being from a socially disadvantaged background damages the prospects of white pupils getting their studies back on track more than for most other ethnic groups.

Summary and conclusion

The aim of this chapter was to set the scene for subsequent analyses. One of the key outcomes of disengagement, and a key factor itself for affecting future outcomes such as further learning or employment prospects, is performance at school and the acquisition or otherwise of good qualifications. This chapter has set the scene by identifying who under-achieves at Key stage 3 (age 14) and more importantly at Key stage 4 (age 16).

At Key stage 4 under-achievement can be measured in absolute terms such as the failure to reach some threshold such as five or more good GCSEs, or it can be measured in relative terms, compared to the individuals' performance earlier in their own school career.

The results suggest that girls are less likely to under-achieve than boys in both periods, particularly the later one. With respect to ethnic group, some interesting differences emerge across the two different periods. In the earlier period, between Key stages 2 and 3, it is black pupils (particularly Afro-Caribbean and 'other black' though not African black pupils to the same extent) who are more likely to under-achieve. The lowest rates of under-achievement at this stage are found among Chinese pupils. The ethnicity effects are broadly the same for both boys and girls at this stage. Looking at the later period, between Key stages 3 and 4, allows us to see whether individuals start to under-achieve at this time, having not under-achieved earlier, and whether individuals who did under-achieve earlier manage to stabilise their performance at their new lower level, or whether they under-achieve further leading up to GCSEs at Key stage 4.

The results reveal that the group most likely to under-achieve between Key stages 3 and 4 are white pupils which, combined with the earlier results, suggests that under-achievement among white pupils becomes much more visible between these ages. For black pupils, their performance stabilises somewhat between these ages, suggesting that the real period of concern for any eventual under-achievement is the earlier period between ages 11 and 14. The lowest under-achievement rates between Key stages 3 and 4 are obtained by Indian, Pakistani and Bangladeshi pupils.

The chapter also considered, for those who under-achieved at Key stage 3, not just whether their performance stabilised at the new lower level as described above, but whether they managed to turn their performance around, and get back up to the level predicted by their Key stage 2 results, by the time they take their GCSEs. The results reveal some very large differences, with boys being much less likely to turn their performance around in this way, and similarly for white pupils. The ethnic groups most likely to get their performances back on track after earlier under-achievement are Indian, Pakistani, Bangladeshi and Chinese pupils. In addition, there are strong interaction effects between gender and ethnicity, suggesting that girls within many of these ethnic groups are much more likely to improve their performance than boys.

Finally, the results showed that, at both points in their school careers (Key stages 3 and 4), pupils who receive free school meals (as an indicator of social background) and pupils with special educational needs are much more likely to under-achieve in their Key stage tests. However, this negative effect of being from a socially deprived background is much stronger for white British pupils than for many other ethnic groups.

Thus the results presented here reveal certain 'at-risk' groups, at whom policy can be focused. With respect to ethnicity, it needs to be understood why the problem period for black pupils seems to be between the ages of 11 and 14, while for white pupils it is more likely to occur between the ages of 14 and 16. White, British-born boys seem particularly likely to under-achieve in the latter age group, or fail to raise their performance then if they have under-achieved earlier. Finally, under-achievement appears to be associated with poorer social backgrounds, and until this is tackled, social mobility and chances to break the poverty cycle for these under-achievers are unlikely to improve.

Regression appendix

Table A2.1
Determinants of under-achievement at Key stage 3
identified on the basis of Key stage 2 results
Data source: Pupil Level Annual School Census/National Pupil Database
Robust standard errors are shown in parentheses
* = Coefficient significant at 5%   ** = Coefficient significant at 1%

Variable	1 Marginal effect (standard error)	2 Marginal effect (standard error)	Number of observations in cell
Female	−0.002 (0.001)*	−0.003 (0.001)*	222,645
Other white	−0.006 (0.005)	−0.014 (0.007)*	6,486
Mixed race	0.008 (0.004)	0.014 (0.007)	7,380
Indian	−0.045 (0.003)**	−0.048 (0.005)**	11,305
Pakistani	0.004 (0.004)	0.024 (0.007)**	8,501
Bangladeshi	0.010 (0.006)	0.034 (0.014)*	3,398
Chinese	−0.104 (0.006)**	−0.116 (0.009)**	1,438
Other Asian	−0.047 (0.007)**	−0.045 (0.012)**	1,837
Afro-Caribbean black	0.094 (0.006)**	0.132 (0.010)**	5,647
African black	0.027 (0.007)**	0.058 (0.012)**	3,476
Other black	0.088 (0.011)**	0.106 (0.018)**	1,579
Other	−0.025 (0.007)**	−0.007 (0.012)	2,247
In receipt of free school meals	0.104 (0.002)**	0.115 (0.003)**	46,122
SEN without statement	0.154 (0.003)**	0.156 (0.003)**	33,300
SEN with statement	0.132 (0.008)**	0.126 (0.009)**	3,387
Female* other white		0.022 (0.010)*	3,306
Female* mixed race		−0.007 (0.008)	4,041
Female* Indian		0.016 (0.008)	5,700
Female* Pakistani		0.004 (0.008)	4,168
Female* Bangladeshi		0.005 (0.012)	1,770
Female* Chinese		0.044 (0.031)	683
Female* other Asian		0.007 (0.019)	926
Female* Afro-Caribbean black		−0.020 (0.008)*	3,071
Female* African black		−0.020 (0.011)	1,880
Female* other black		0.010 (0.017)	829
Female* other		−0.009 (0.015)	1,091
SEN (with)* other white		0.031 (0.057)	41
SEN (with)* mixed race		0.101 (0.051)*	70
SEN (with)* Indian		−0.004 (0.054)	42
SEN (with)* Pakistani		0.009 (0.048)	49
SEN (with)* Bangladeshi		0.048 (0.098)	14
SEN (with)* Chinese		0.003 (0.138)	9
SEN (with)* other Asian		−0.049 (0.117)	6
SEN (with)* Afro-Caribbean black		−0.024 (0.043)	46
SEN (with)* African black		0.110 (0.086)	24
SEN (with)* other black		−0.007 (0.098)	10

Variable	1 Marginal effect (standard error)	2 Marginal effect (standard error)		Number of observations in cell
SEN (with)* other		0.011	(0.070)	24
SEN (without)* other white		−0.003	(0.014)	625
SEN (without)* mixed race		−0.023	(0.012)	724
SEN (without)* Indian		0.008	(0.014)	654
SEN (without)* Pakistani		0.006	(0.013)	696
SEN (without)* Bangladeshi		0.009	(0.021)	270
SEN (without)* Chinese		0.037	(0.052)	72
SEN (without)* other Asian		−0.022	(0.030)	117
SEN (without)* Afro-Caribbean black		−0.023	(0.011)*	875
SEN (without)* African black		−0.021	(0.015)	446
SEN (without)* other black		−0.018	(0.021)	446
SEN (without)* other		−0.048	(0.020)*	216
Free school meals* other white		−0.013	(0.012)	838
Free school meals* mixed race		−0.007	(0.010)	1,489
Free school meals* Indian		−0.030	(0.010)*	1,267
Free school meals* Pakistani		−0.052	(0.006)**	3,190
Free school meals* Bangladeshi		−0.041	(0.010)**	2,154
Free school meals* Chinese		0.008	(0.034)	191
Free school meals* other Asian		−0.026	(0.021)	312
Free school meals* Afro-Caribbean black		−0.048	(0.008)**	1,427
Free school meals* African black		−0.037	(0.010)**	1,217
Free school meals* other black		−0.052	(0.014)**	429
Free school meals* other		−0.032	(0.015)*	616
Observations	413,149	413,149		413,149

Table A2.2
Determinants of under-achievement at Key stage 4
identified on the basis of Key stage 3 results
Data source: Pupil Level Annual School Census/National Pupil Database
Robust standard errors are shown in parentheses
* = Coefficient significant at 5% ** = Coefficient significant at 1%

Variable	1 Marginal effect (standard error)		2 Marginal effect (standard error)	
Female	−0.056	(0.001)**	−0.056	(0.001)**
Other white	−0.030	(0.003)**	−0.030	(0.005)**
Mixed race	−0.002	(0.003)	0.006	(0.006)
Indian	−0.080	(0.002)**	−0.068	(0.003)**
Pakistani	−0.083	(0.002)**	−0.056	(0.004)**
Bangladeshi	−0.085	(0.002)**	−0.048	(0.008)**
Chinese	−0.056	(0.005)**	−0.039	(0.009)**
Other Asian	−0.068	(0.004)**	−0.057	(0.007)**
Afro-Caribbean black	−0.024	(0.003)**	0.005	(0.007)
African black	−0.079	(0.002)**	−0.049	(0.006)**
Other black	−0.004	(0.007)	0.007	(0.012)
Other	−0.041	(0.005)**	−0.014	(0.009)
In receipt of free school meals	0.094	(0.002)**	0.112	(0.002)**
SEN without statement	0.123	(0.002)**	0.129	(0.002)**
SEN with statement	0.096	(0.006)**	0.093	(0.006)**
Female* other white			0.020	(0.008)*
Female* mixed race			0.001	(0.007)
Female* Indian			−0.019	(0.007)**
Female* Pakistani			−0.029	(0.007)**
Female* Bangladeshi			−0.031	(0.010)**
Female* Chinese			−0.014	(0.017)
Female* other Asian			0.001	(0.017)
Female* Afro-Caribbean black			−0.006	(0.008)
Female* African black			−0.013	(0.010)
Female* other black			0.010	(0.015)
Female* other			0.009	(0.013)
SEN (with)* other white			0.054	(0.037)
SEN (with)* mixed race			0.015	(0.028)
SEN (with)* Indian			0.006	(0.037)
SEN (with)* Pakistani			0.002	(0.031)
SEN (with)* Bangladeshi			0.003	(0.052)
SEN (with)* Chinese			−0.007	(0.079)
SEN (with)* other Asian				
SEN (with)* Afro-Caribbean black			0.047	(0.036)
SEN (with)* African black			−0.076	(0.029)**
SEN (with)* other black			0.041	(0.072)

Variable	1 Marginal effect (standard error)	2 Marginal effect (standard error)
SEN (with)* other		0.004 (0.051)
SEN (without)* other white		−0.006 (0.010)
SEN (without)* mixed race		−0.013 (0.009)
SEN (without)* Indian		−0.046 (0.009)**
SEN (without)* Pakistani		−0.048 (0.008)**
SEN (without)* Bangladeshi		−0.036 (0.013)**
SEN (without)* Chinese		−0.046 (0.022)*
SEN (without)* other Asian		−0.036 (0.020)
SEN (without)* Afro-Caribbean black		−0.024 (0.008)**
SEN (without)* African black		−0.035 (0.010)**
SEN (without)* other black		−0.016 (0.016)
SEN (without)* other		−0.020 (0.015)
Free school meals* other white		−0.042 (0.007)**
Free school meals* mixed race		−0.030 (0.006)**
Free school meals* Indian		−0.056 (0.007)**
Free school meals* Pakistani		−0.061 (0.005)**
Free school meals* Bangladeshi		−0.064 (0.007)**
Free school meals* Chinese		−0.072 (0.013)**
Free school meals* other Asian		−0.049 (0.013)**
Free school meals* Afro-Caribbean black		−0.065 (0.005)**
Free school meals* African black		−0.074 (0.005)**
Free school meals* other black		−0.043 (0.011)**
Free school meals* other		−0.076 (0.006)**
Observations	454,474	454,461

Table A2.3
Determinants of under-achievement at Key stage 4
identified on the basis of Key stage 3 results
and failure to acquire five or more good GCSEs
Data source: Pupil Level Annual School Census/National Pupil Database
Robust standard errors are shown in parentheses
* = Coefficient significant at 5%   ** = Coefficient significant at 1%

Variable	1 Marginal effect (standard error)		2 Marginal effect (standard error)	
Female	−0.040	(0.001)**	−0.039	(0.001)**
Other white	−0.023	(0.003)**	−0.023	(0.004)**
Mixed race	−0.005	(0.003)	0.002	(0.005)
Indian	−0.067	(0.001)**	−0.059	(0.002)**
Pakistani	−0.064	(0.001)**	−0.041	(0.003)**
Bangladeshi	−0.066	(0.002)**	−0.036	(0.007)**
Chinese	−0.053	(0.004)**	−0.046	(0.007)**
Other Asian	−0.054	(0.003)**	−0.047	(0.006)**
Afro-Caribbean black	−0.013	(0.003)**	0.022	(0.006)**
African black	−0.062	(0.002)**	−0.032	(0.005)**
Other black	0.004	(0.006)	0.023	(0.011)*
Other	−0.033	(0.004)**	−0.009	(0.008)
In receipt of free school meals	0.101	(0.002)**	0.119	(0.002)**
SEN without statement	0.139	(0.002)**	0.145	(0.002)**
SEN with statement	0.117	(0.005)**	0.114	(0.006)**
Female* other white			0.023	(0.008)**
Female* mixed race			0.001	(0.006)
Female* Indian			−0.013	(0.007)
Female* Pakistani			−0.021	(0.006)**
Female* Bangladeshi			−0.022	(0.009)*
Female* Chinese			0.003	(0.018)
Female* other Asian			0.010	(0.016)
Female* Afro-Caribbean black			−0.009	(0.006)
Female* African black			−0.015	(0.008)
Female* other black			0.003	(0.012)
Female* other			0.011	(0.012)
SEN (with)* other white			0.042	(0.031)
SEN (with)* mixed race			0.020	(0.024)
SEN (with)* Indian			0.015	(0.034)
SEN (with)* Pakistani			0.000	(0.025)
SEN (with)* Bangladeshi			0.000	(0.042)
SEN (with)* Chinese			−0.033	(0.055)
SEN (with)* other Asian				
SEN (with)* Afro-Caribbean black			0.031	(0.029)
SEN (with)* African black			−0.058	(0.022)**
SEN (with)* other black			0.026	(0.057)

Variable	1 Marginal effect (standard error)	2 Marginal effect (standard error)
SEN (with)* other		0.003 (0.042)
SEN (without)* other white		−0.006 (0.008)
SEN (without)* mixed race		−0.012 (0.007)
SEN (without)* Indian		−0.026 (0.008)**
SEN (without)* Pakistani		−0.040 (0.006)**
SEN (without)* Bangladeshi		−0.034 (0.010)**
SEN (without)* Chinese		−0.018 (0.022)
SEN (without)* other Asian		−0.029 (0.016)
SEN (without)* Afro-Caribbean black		−0.026 (0.006)**
SEN (without)* African black		−0.028 (0.008)**
SEN (without)* other black		−0.024 (0.011)*
SEN (without)* other		−0.025 (0.011)*
Free school meals* other white		−0.039 (0.005)**
Free school meals* mixed race		−0.022 (0.005)**
Free school meals* Indian		−0.045 (0.006)**
Free school meals* Pakistani		−0.051 (0.004)**
Free school meals* Bangladeshi		−0.052 (0.005)**
Free school meals* Chinese		−0.052 (0.012)**
Free school meals* other Asian		−0.038 (0.011)**
Free school meals* Afro-Caribbean black		−0.058 (0.003)**
Free school meals* African black		−0.064 (0.004)**
Free school meals* other black		−0.036 (0.008)**
Free school meals* other		−0.059 (0.005)**
Observations	454,474	454,461

Table A2.4
Determinants of under-achievement at Key stage 4
identified on the basis of Key stage 3 results
and failure to acquire five or more GCSEs at any grade
Data source: Pupil Level Annual School Census/National Pupil Database
Robust standard errors are shown in parentheses
* = Coefficient significant at 5% ** = Coefficient significant at 1%

Variable	1 Marginal effect (standard error)		2 Marginal effect (standard error)	
Female	-0.003	(0.001)**	-0.003	(0.001)**
Other white	-0.003	(0.002)	0.003	(0.003)
Mixed race	-0.000	(0.002)	0.007	(0.003)*
Indian	-0.027	(0.001)**	-0.024	(0.001)**
Pakistani	-0.023	(0.001)**	-0.009	(0.003)**
Bangladeshi	-0.024	(0.001)**	-0.001	(0.006)
Chinese	-0.016	(0.003)**	-0.007	(0.006)
Other Asian	-0.018	(0.002)**	-0.015	(0.004)**
Afro-Caribbean black	-0.006	(0.002)**	0.018	(0.005)**
African black	-0.022	(0.001)**	0.002	(0.005)
Other black	0.011	(0.004)**	0.037	(0.010)**
Other	-0.008	(0.002)**	0.009	(0.006)
In receipt of free school meals	0.056	(0.001)**	0.065	(0.001)**
SEN without statement	0.104	(0.002)**	0.110	(0.002)**
SEN with statement	0.129	(0.005)**	0.130	(0.005)**
Female* other white			0.005	(0.004)
Female* mixed race			-0.002	(0.003)
Female* Indian			-0.000	(0.005)
Female* Pakistani			-0.008	(0.003)*
Female* Bangladeshi			-0.012	(0.004)**
Female* Chinese			0.002	(0.011)
Female* other Asian			0.008	(0.010)
Female* Afro-Caribbean black			-0.012	(0.003)**
Female* African black			-0.011	(0.004)**
Female* other black			-0.011	(0.005)*
Female* other			0.001	(0.006)
SEN (with)* other white			0.002	(0.012)
SEN (with)* mixed race			-0.003	(0.009)
SEN (with)* Indian			0.024	(0.022)
SEN (with)* Pakistani			-0.015	(0.008)*
SEN (with)* Bangladeshi			-0.007	(0.017)
SEN (with)* Chinese				
SEN (with)* other Asian				
SEN (with)* Afro-Caribbean black			0.018	(0.016)
SEN (with)* African black			-0.024	(0.007)**
SEN (with)* other black			0.003	(0.024)

Variable	1 Marginal effect (standard error)	2 Marginal effect (standard error)
SEN (with)* other		0.003 (0.020)
SEN (without)* other white		−0.011 (0.003)**
SEN (without)* mixed race		−0.012 (0.003)**
SEN (without)* Indian		−0.013 (0.004)**
SEN (without)* Pakistani		−0.019 (0.002)**
SEN (without)* Bangladeshi		−0.022 (0.003)**
SEN (without)* Chinese		−0.012 (0.010)
SEN (without)* other Asian		−0.019 (0.006)**
SEN (without)* Afro-Caribbean black		−0.011 (0.003)**
SEN (without)* African black		−0.019 (0.003)**
SEN (without)* other black		−0.014 (0.005)**
SEN (without)* other		−0.012 (0.005)*
Free school meals* other white		−0.016 (0.002)**
Free school meals* mixed race		−0.008 (0.003)**
Free school meals* Indian		−0.018 (0.003)**
Free school meals* Pakistani		−0.021 (0.002)**
Free school meals* Bangladeshi		−0.024 (0.002)**
Free school meals* Chinese		−0.031 (0.001)**
Free school meals* other Asian		−0.012 (0.006)*
Free school meals* Afro-Caribbean black		−0.022 (0.002)**
Free school meals* African black		−0.026 (0.001)**
Free school meals* other black		−0.016 (0.004)**
Free school meals* other		−0.023 (0.002)**
Observations	454,474	454,447

Table A2.5
Determinants of under-achievement at Key stage 4
identified on the basis of Key stage 2 results
if under-achieved at Key stage 3
Data source: Pupil Level Annual School Census/National Pupil Database
Robust standard errors are shown in parentheses
* = Coefficient significant at 5% ** = Coefficient significant at 1%

Variable	1 Marginal effect (standard error)		2 Marginal effect (standard error)	
Female	−0.113	(0.004)**	−0.108	(0.004)**
Other white	−0.060	(0.014)**	−0.036	(0.023)
Mixed race	−0.021	(0.013)	−0.008	(0.021)
Indian	−0.199	(0.010)**	−0.184	(0.016)**
Pakistani	−0.226	(0.008)**	−0.181	(0.016)**
Bangladeshi	−0.226	(0.012)**	−0.086	(0.035)*
Chinese	−0.233	(0.034)**	−0.158	(0.072)*
Other Asian	−0.146	(0.027)**	−0.108	(0.046)*
Afro-Caribbean black	−0.057	(0.011)**	0.010	(0.020)
African black	−0.182	(0.013)**	−0.116	(0.027)**
Other black	−0.017	(0.022)	0.042	(0.038)
Other	−0.112	(0.022)**	−0.010	(0.040)
In receipt of free school meals	0.127	(0.005)**	0.149	(0.006)**
SEN without statement	0.153	(0.005)**	0.157	(0.006)**
SEN with statement	0.063	(0.017)**	0.057	(0.018)**
Female* other white			0.030	(0.031)
Female* mixed race			0.021	(0.027)
Female* Indian			−0.006	(0.030)
Female* Pakistani			−0.092	(0.025)**
Female* Bangladeshi			−0.140	(0.032)**
Female* Chinese			−0.120	(0.107)
Female* other Asian			−0.004	(0.069)
Female* Afro-Caribbean black			−0.056	(0.023)*
Female* African black			−0.083	(0.034)*
Female* other black			−0.113	(0.040)**
Female* other			−0.086	(0.048)
SEN (with)* other white			0.176	(0.141)
SEN (with)* mixed race			−0.076	(0.081)
SEN (with)* Indian			0.249	(0.161)
SEN (with)* Pakistani			0.166	(0.134)
SEN (with)* Bangladeshi			0.125	(0.214)
SEN (with)* Chinese				
SEN (with)* other Asian				
SEN (with)* Afro-Caribbean black			0.076	(0.121)
SEN (with)* African black			−0.153	(0.127)
SEN (with)* other black			0.217	(0.266)

Variable	1 Marginal effect (standard error)	2 Marginal effect (standard error)
SEN (with)* other		−0.063 (0.177)
SEN (without)* other white		−0.057 (0.036)
SEN (without)* mixed race		−0.003 (0.035)
SEN (without)* Indian		−0.007 (0.042)
SEN (without)* Pakistani		−0.044 (0.034)
SEN (without)* Bangladeshi		−0.073 (0.050)
SEN (without)* Chinese		−0.088 (0.145)
SEN (without)* other Asian		−0.011 (0.100)
SEN (without)* Afro-Caribbean black		−0.038 (0.027)
SEN (without)* African black		0.025 (0.045)
SEN (without)* other black		0.058 (0.059)
SEN (without)* other		−0.056 (0.069)
Free school meals* other white		−0.140 (0.030)**
Free school meals* mixed race		−0.078 (0.026)**
Free school meals* Indian		−0.109 (0.034)**
Free school meals* Pakistani		−0.058 (0.026)*
Free school meals* Bangladeshi		−0.152 (0.033)**
Free school meals* Chinese		−0.128 (0.113)
Free school meals* other Asian		−0.149 (0.062)*
Free school meals* Afro-Caribbean black		−0.107 (0.023)**
Free school meals* African black		−0.117 (0.032)**
Free school meals* other black		−0.047 (0.047)
Free school meals* other		−0.158 (0.042)**
Observations	69,484	69,482

Table A2.6
Determinants of under-achievement at Key stage 4
identified on the basis of Key stage 2 results
and failure to acquire five or more good GCSEs
if under-achieved at Key stage 3
Data source: Pupil Level Annual School Census/National Pupil Database
Robust standard errors are shown in parentheses
* = Coefficient significant at 5%   ** = Coefficient significant at 1%

Variable	1 Marginal effect (standard error)		2 Marginal effect (standard error)	
Female	−0.099	(0.004)**	−0.093	(0.004)**
Other white	−0.055	(0.013)**	−0.031	(0.023)
Mixed race	−0.019	(0.012)	−0.001	(0.021)
Indian	−0.186	(0.010)**	−0.162	(0.016)**
Pakistani	−0.203	(0.008)**	−0.154	(0.016)**
Bangladeshi	−0.205	(0.011)**	−0.046	(0.036)
Chinese	−0.245	(0.027)**	−0.179	(0.064)**
Other Asian	−0.149	(0.025)**	−0.086	(0.045)
Afro-Caribbean black	−0.042	(0.011)**	0.033	(0.020)
African black	−0.166	(0.012)**	−0.088	(0.027)**
Other black	−0.017	(0.022)	0.058	(0.038)
Other	−0.104	(0.021)**	−0.001	(0.040)
In receipt of free school meals	0.143	(0.005)**	0.167	(0.006)**
SEN without statement	0.184	(0.005)**	0.189	(0.006)**
SEN with statement	0.103	(0.017)**	0.098	(0.018)**
Female* other white			0.025	(0.030)
Female* mixed race			0.018	(0.026)
Female* Indian			−0.037	(0.029)
Female* Pakistani			−0.099	(0.023)**
Female* Bangladeshi			−0.153	(0.028)**
Female* Chinese			−0.142	(0.109)
Female* other Asian			−0.072	(0.063)
Female* Afro-Caribbean black			−0.054	(0.022)*
Female* African black			−0.088	(0.032)**
Female* other black			−0.109	(0.037)**
Female* other			−0.088	(0.045)
SEN (with)* other white			0.171	(0.142)
SEN (with)* mixed race			−0.068	(0.077)
SEN (with)* Indian			0.251	(0.165)
SEN (with)* Pakistani			0.148	(0.134)
SEN (with)* Bangladeshi			0.110	(0.211)
SEN (with)* Chinese				
SEN (with)* other Asian				
SEN (with)* Afro-Caribbean black			0.063	(0.117)
SEN (with)* African black			−0.152	(0.112)
SEN (with)* other black			0.203	(0.270)

Variable	1 Marginal effect (standard error)	2 Marginal effect (standard error)
SEN (with)* other		−0.057 (0.167)
SEN (without)* other white		−0.052 (0.034)
SEN (without)* mixed race		0.005 (0.034)
SEN (without)* Indian		0.006 (0.041)
SEN (without)* Pakistani		−0.054 (0.032)
SEN (without)* Bangladeshi		−0.074 (0.046)
SEN (without)* Chinese		0.026 (0.169)
SEN (without)* other Asian		−0.028 (0.095)
SEN (without)* Afro-Caribbean black		−0.043 (0.026)
SEN (without)* African black		−0.005 (0.042)
SEN (without)* other black		−0.011 (0.053)
SEN (without)* other		−0.047 (0.066)
Free school meals* other white		−0.130 (0.027)**
Free school meals* mixed race		−0.091 (0.024)**
Free school meals* Indian		−0.108 (0.032)**
Free school meals* Pakistani		−0.060 (0.025)*
Free school meals* Bangladeshi		−0.164 (0.028)**
Free school meals* Chinese		−0.205 (0.089)*
Free school meals* other Asian		−0.143 (0.058)*
Free school meals* Afro-Caribbean black		−0.121 (0.020)**
Free school meals* African black		−0.126 (0.029)**
Free school meals* other black		−0.052 (0.044)
Free school meals* other		−0.156 (0.038)**
Observations	69,484	69,482

Table A2.7
Determinants of under-achievement at Key stage 4
identified on the basis of Key stage 2 results
and failure to acquire five or more GCSEs at any grade
if under-achieved at Key stage 3
Data source: Pupil Level Annual School Census/National Pupil Database
Robust standard errors are shown in parentheses
* = Coefficient significant at 5%   ** = Coefficient significant at 1%

Variable	1 Marginal effect (standard error)		2 Marginal effect (standard error)	
Female	−0.008	(0.002)**	−0.006	(0.002)*
Other white	−0.002	(0.008)	0.016	(0.016)
Mixed race	−0.009	(0.007)	0.015	(0.014)
Indian	−0.062	(0.004)**	−0.051	(0.009)**
Pakistani	−0.063	(0.003)**	−0.042	(0.010)**
Bangladeshi	−0.069	(0.004)**	−0.017	(0.023)
Chinese	−0.073	(0.011)**	−0.061	(0.030)*
Other Asian	−0.060	(0.010)**	−0.046	(0.022)*
Afro-Caribbean black	−0.030	(0.005)**	0.000	(0.012)
African black	−0.064	(0.005)**	−0.040	(0.014)**
Other black	0.008	(0.013)	0.029	(0.025)
Other	−0.031	(0.011)**	0.001	(0.025)
In receipt of free school meals	0.079	(0.004)**	0.089	(0.004)**
SEN without statement	0.159	(0.004)**	0.165	(0.005)**
SEN with statement	0.149	(0.014)**	0.143	(0.015)**
Female* other white			0.005	(0.017)
Female* mixed race			−0.015	(0.013)
Female* Indian			−0.002	(0.021)
Female* Pakistani			−0.030	(0.013)*
Female* Bangladeshi			−0.061	(0.011)**
Female* Chinese			−0.003	(0.102)
Female* other Asian			0.009	(0.054)
Female* Afro-Caribbean black			−0.029	(0.011)**
Female* African black			−0.031	(0.019)
Female* other black			−0.031	(0.018)
Female* other			0.014	(0.034)
SEN (with)* other white			0.153	(0.111)
SEN (with)* mixed race			−0.035	(0.029)
SEN (with)* Indian			0.114	(0.133)
SEN (with)* Pakistani				
SEN (with)* Bangladeshi			0.073	(0.146)
SEN (with)* Chinese				
SEN (with)* other Asian				
SEN (with)* Afro-Caribbean black			0.232	(0.110)*
SEN (with)* African black			−0.022	(0.068)
SEN (with)* other black			−0.020	(0.087)

Variable	1 Marginal effect (standard error)	2 Marginal effect (standard error)
SEN (with)* other		-0.028 (0.070)
SEN (without)* other white		-0.026 (0.014)
SEN (without)* mixed race		-0.027 (0.013)*
SEN (without)* Indian		-0.037 (0.017)*
SEN (without)* Pakistani		-0.043 (0.012)**
SEN (without)* Bangladeshi		-0.032 (0.022)
SEN (without)* Chinese		0.055 (0.159)
SEN (without)* other Asian		-0.040 (0.039)
SEN (without)* Afro-Caribbean black		-0.016 (0.013)
SEN (without)* African black		0.001 (0.027)
SEN (without)* other black		0.013 (0.029)
SEN (without)* other		-0.013 (0.032)
Free school meals* other white		-0.047 (0.011)**
Free school meals* mixed race		-0.018 (0.013)
Free school meals* Indian		-0.043 (0.016)**
Free school meals* Pakistani		-0.023 (0.014)
Free school meals* Bangladeshi		-0.055 (0.013)**
Free school meals* Chinese		
Free school meals* other Asian		-0.054 (0.027)*
Free school meals* Afro-Caribbean black		-0.041 (0.009)**
Free school meals* African black		-0.053 (0.012)**
Free school meals* other black		-0.013 (0.022)
Free school meals* other		-0.064 (0.011)**
Observations	69,484	69,442

3 Disengagement: truancy in the Youth Cohort Study

Introduction

Having provided a description of under-achievement in the previous chapter, this chapter focuses on the main topic of this research study, namely disengagement. It is being argued that disengagement from the education process may be responsible for some of the under-achievement discussed in the previous chapter this relationship will be investigated in the next chapter). Again, it should be stressed that it is not being claimed that the only reason for under-achievement is disengagement, nor is it being argued that disengagement at some point during a school career will automatically lead to poor performance and under-achievement in final exams. There will be many other causes of under-achievement and many other consequences of disengagement. However, this relationship is the focus of the present study, and the association between the two concepts will be developed in the next chapter. For now, this chapter describes factors associated with disengagement, with the aim of building up a picture of disengaged individuals, in terms of their personal characteristics such as gender and ethnicity, but also in terms of their family background, and some characteristics of their school. Such an analysis could be helpful in eventually explaining why disengagement occurs.

The indicator of disengagement to be used in this study is the frequency of truancy. Again it must be stressed, as discussed in the Introduction, that it is not being claimed that pupils' absence from school suggests that they are disengaged, nor that the only representation of disengagement is truancy. Those who are absent from school may be fulfilling other roles such as caring for family members, rather than simply disengaging from school. Similarly, those who are disengaged may turn up for school, but make no effort once they are there. We therefore use truancy data only because it represents the best data on disengagement available in large, national data sets, and it should at least be strongly correlated with disengagement, even if it is not an exact representation.

The data set and the truancy variable

The Youth Cohort Study

The data set used is the Youth Cohort Study (YCS). This is a series of nationally representative surveys of cohorts of 16 year olds, who are then followed up and surveyed again a further two times, either annually or bi-annually. So far, 11 cohorts of initially young people have been surveyed, with the data from the first 10 currently being available. This study uses data from the first sweeps of the surveys of Cohorts 8, 9 and 10, undertaken in 1996, 1998 and 2000 respectively. The sampled individuals are obviously completely different across cohorts, so this study is using three completely separate data sets. The reason for studying three different cohorts is to investigate whether results are replicated across cohorts. If the same results continue to emerge for each cohort, we can have confidence that such results are genuine findings observed across different groups of people, and are not merely chance observations.

The truancy variable

The question on truancy is the same for each cohort, and asks respondents to self-report how often they played truant. Specifically, the questions asks:

Thinking back to Year 11 (fifth year), did you play truant from school:

	Cohort 8	Cohort 9	Cohort 10
1 for weeks at a time	1.8%	1.7%	1.3%
2 for several days at a time	1.8%	2.0%	1.5%
3 for particular days or lessons	5.7%	5.5%	4.9%
4 for the odd day or lesson	26.7%	25.7%	24.2%
5 never?	64.1%	65.2%	68.1%

Data source: Youth Cohort Study

The obvious point to make about this variable is its self-reported nature. Answers to such questions may not equate with the truth, either because of forgetfulness or deliberate lying. In statistical regression techniques, such measurement error in the dependent variable does not actually bias any results, but only reduces their precision, assuming that the measurement error is unrelated to any of the explanatory variables in the estimated equation, but is randomly distributed across individuals. This assumption will not hold if particular subgroups of the sample are more likely to forget or lie. For example, it could be imagined that boys might be more likely than girls to want to boast about their truancy, and so in this case the measurement error (over-reporting by boys and under-reporting by girls) is systematically related to one of the explanatory variables, namely gender, and the resulting coefficients would be biased. In actual fact, as we will soon see, girls actually report higher rates of truancy than boys, so this line of reasoning does not seem to be relevant here. Of course, there is no way of knowing whether the incidence of forgetfulness or lying is indeed systematically related to any of the characteristics of individuals considered here, since of course we do not know the true incidence of truancy. The analysis will therefore proceed on the assumption that there is no measurement error, or it is distributed randomly across individuals, on the basis of a lack of theoretical reasons for the contrary.

Other variables

The YCS has a range of other information that can be used as control or explanatory variables in the estimated model. This list of variables includes gender, ethnicity, family status (parental occupation and ownership of home), family composition (presence of both parents in family home and number of siblings), region of residence and indicators of school quality (school type, average class size, numbers on pupil roll with special educational needs or entitled to free school meals, provision of careers advice and work experience). In addition, the extended questionnaire administered to Cohort 10 respondents helps us to identify and control for other background factors, such as respondents' own SEN status, whether they have ever been in social care and the extent of parental interest in their education.

Table A3.1 in the Regression Appendix to this chapter provides some basic descriptive statistics, displaying the distribution of the sampled individuals across their various different characteristics.

Truancy rates by characteristics of the respondents

Table 3.1 and Figure 3.1 present information on the truancy rate for various groups found in the data, according to the variables just described. It was first decided to collapse the five-point response scale described above into a yes/no truancy indicator, to aid clarity of presentation. For Figure 3.1, the cut-off point was defined between those who had never played truant, and those who had, regardless of frequency or severity. Defining the disengaged as only the more serious truants, and what difference this makes to the results, will be considered later.

Table 3.1
Differences in the truancy rate across sample characteristics
Data source: Youth Cohort Study

	Truancy rate
Cohort 8	35.9
Cohort 9	34.8
Cohort 10	31.9
Pupil variables	
Male	29.7
Female	33.7
White	32.1
Black	36.8
Asian	28.5
Other ethnic groups	31.8
Family variables	
Father in senior occupation	25.9
Father in non-senior occupation	35.5
Mother in senior occupation	27.6
Mother in non-senior occupation	33.6
Father present	29.4
No father present	43.4
Mother present	30.8
No mother present	47.5
Privately owned home	29.2
Renting	44.5

Figure 3.1
Differences in the truancy rate across sample characteristics
Data source: Youth Cohort Study

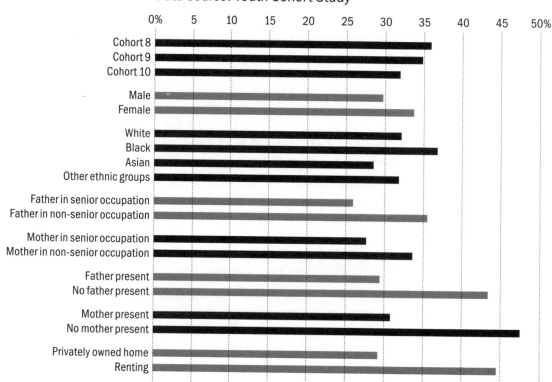

The first bars in Figure 3.1 show the rate of truancy among all respondents in each of the three cohorts considered. Beyond these first bars, only data from Cohort 10 is used to show how the truancy rate varies by characteristics of individuals, in order to keep the diagram simple to read. The pattern of results is not significantly altered if another cohort, or the average of all three, is used.

Reading from left to right, then, the first three bars show quite a steady level of self-reported truancy, with about one-third of each of the cohorts studied reporting playing truant at some point in Year 11. The actual truancy rate declines in each successive cohort, though by such small amounts that probably not much should be made of this.

The next two bars show that, perhaps surprisingly, a higher proportion of girls than boys report playing truant. The difference is not large but would show up in each of the three cohorts studied if results from each were graphed. This is somewhat of a surprise, and is in contrast with most administrative records on truancy, which report higher rates among boys. It may be that the self-reported nature of the data is affecting the results in this case, with perhaps girls being more truthful about their truancy behaviour than boys. The next group of bars consider the individuals' ethnic identity. The results suggest that black pupils have the highest truancy rate and Asian pupils the lowest, with white pupils and other ethnic groups falling in between.

The remaining bars in Figure 3.1 consider aspects of the respondents' family background, rather than their own characteristics. The results show large differences in truancy rates across different types of households. Thus individuals in households in which one of the parents is in a senior occupation[17] have a lower truancy rate. The difference seems to be particularly marked between households with and without a senior occupation father (truancy rates of 26% and 36% respectively). The absence of either parent[18] is also strongly related to truancy, and in this case it is the absence of the mother that seems to make the most difference. Thus almost half (48%) of respondents not living with their mother report playing truant in Year 11, compared to 31% of those who do live with their mother. The final bars again show a very large difference in truancy rates across types of house occupancy, intended to proxy for social class, with 29% of those living in a privately owned home reporting playing truant, compared to 45% of those living in a rented home.

As described earlier, the above results refer to reported rates of truancy, no matter how serious the degree of truancy. It could be that certain groups are more likely to miss occasional days, but do not display more serious disengagement by regularly and systematically missing particular lessons, or truanting for extended periods.[19] For example, perhaps the gender results observed above reflect the fact that girls are more prone to take the occasional day off, while leaving the serious truanting to the boys. The results in Table 3.2 and Figure 3.2, however, show that this is not the case.

Table 3.2
Differences in the serious truancy rate across sample characteristics
Data source: Youth Cohort Study

	Serious truancy rate
Cohort 8	9.2
Cohort 9	9.2
Cohort 10	7.7
Pupil variables	
Male	7.3
Female	8.1
White	7.7
Black	12.3
Asian	6.9
Other ethnic groups	7.0
Family variables	
Father in senior occupation	4.5
Father in non-senior occupation	9.7
Mother in senior occupation	5.7
Mother in non-senior occupation	8.5
Father present	6.3
No father present	14.3
Mother present	7.1
No mother present	17.4
Privately owned home	5.8
Renting	16.5

17
Senior occupations are defined as the first three major groups in the Standard Occupational Classification, namely managers, professionals and associate professionals.

18
Strictly speaking, this should read the absence of a parent figure, since the survey question asks respondents whether they live with a father or stepfather, and a mother or stepmother. Note also that this question asks respondents for their household composition at the time of the survey, not in the period for which they are asked to report any truancy (ie Year 11).

19
Thus, for this definition of serious truancy, the cut-off point in the scale used for the truancy question, reprinted above, is after point 3 ('for particular days or lessons'), so that point 4 ('for the odd day or lesson') is not considered to be serious truancy. It has been suggested that the serious truants should be defined as only the top two categories, ie playing truant for weeks at a time or days at a time. However the numbers in these groups were too small for statistical analysis, and so it was decided to keep those individuals regularly playing truant for particular days or lessons in the definition of serious truants.

Figure 3.2
Differences in the serious truancy rate across sample characteristics
Data source: Youth Cohort Study

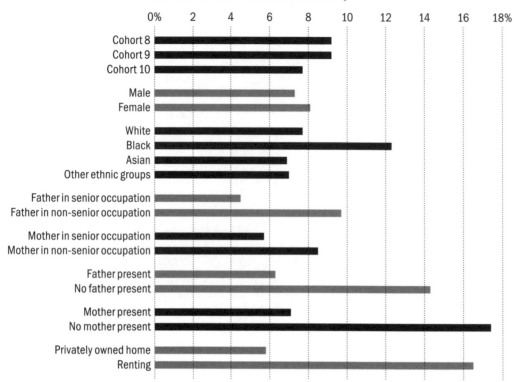

Even when only serious truanting is considered, girls are still slightly more likely to engage in such behaviour than boys, or at least to self-report more truancy. For every other characteristic of individuals and their families, the same pattern of results also holds for serious truancy as it did for any truancy. Some of the differences are quite dramatic, such as the rate of serious truancy among those who live in rented accommodation being almost three times that of individuals who live in privately owned homes (17% compared with 6%).

Key points

Self-reported truancy rates are highest among:

■ girls, somewhat surprisingly, perhaps reflecting their greater honesty rather than their greater truancy, given the results in official records

■ black pupils, followed by white pupils, with Asian pupils having the lowest rates

■ those whose parents work in non-professional jobs (particularly the father)

■ those who do not live with both parents (particularly the absence of the mother).

Multivariate analysis of the factors associated with truancy behaviour

20
The estimation procedure used is actually a probit equation, which, as described in the previous chapter, makes allowance for the fact that the dependent variable, truancy, is a categorical (yes/no) variable, rather than a cardinal variable. The numbers contained in Table A3.2 are marginal effects, ie they represent the percentage point change in the probability of truanting for a unit change in each explanatory variable (or, in the case of categorical explanatory variables, which form the bulk of the equation, the percentage point difference in the probability of truancy between the category indicated by the categorical variable and the omitted category).

21
The variable 'father's occupation missing' is included because for a significant number of the sample, father's occupation is not defined, because they either have no father or their father is not employed. Because statistical packages simply drop observations for which there is a missing value for any of the variables included in the equation, to include father's occupation with many missing values would therefore greatly reduce the number of observations on which the equation is estimated. It is therefore standard practice to change all of the missing values to zeros in the father's occupation variable, and then include the variable 'father's occupation missing' to indicate which observations have made this change. Exactly the same argument is made for the inclusion of the variable 'mother's occupation missing', since a significant number of mothers of sample members do not work.

The analysis, as conducted so far in this chapter, essentially considers cross-tabulations in the data, by looking at the relationship between truancy and one characteristic of individuals at a time in isolation from the other characteristics. To the extent that the various characteristics of individuals are related to one another, this can give misleading results. For example, consider the result that pupils with a father in a senior occupation are less likely to truant. In addition, the results showed that black pupils are more likely to truant. However, if black pupils are less likely to have a father in a professional occupation, then their higher rate of truancy may be due to the socio-economic status of their families, rather than their ethnic origin. We therefore turn now to a regression-based analysis[20] of the determinants of truancy, which has the advantage that it provides estimates of the 'pure' effect of each included variable on truancy, holding constant the influence of all other variables included in the analysis. The results are contained in Table A3.2 in the Regression Appendix.

Many of the results are in fact consistent with the cross-tabulations contained within Table 3.1 and Figure 3.1. Considering them in detail, they show that girls are more likely to have played truant than boys. This result and the size of the effect (a 4–5 percentage point greater probability of truanting) is remarkably consistent across the three cohorts, so this surprising finding is not an anomalous result obtained in a single cross-section of data. Again, we can only hypothesise that it might reflect greater honesty among girls.

The coefficients on the dummy variables indicating ethnic grouping indicate the difference in truancy behaviour between each group included, and the omitted category, which is formed of white pupils. Most of the estimated effects on the ethnicity variables are negative, suggesting that, holding other factors constant, white pupils are more likely to truant than other ethnic groups. Some of these differences in truancy behaviour are statistically significant, namely between black pupils and white pupils in Cohort 9, and between Asian and white pupils in both Cohorts 9 and 10. Thus, the 'other things being equal' assumption is important when considering differences in truancy across ethnic groups, and while the raw data in Table 3.1 and Figure 3.1 suggested that black pupils are more likely to play truant than white pupils, when the family background is held constant, as in Table A3.1, then the results show that black pupils are no more likely to play truant, and if anything are less likely to play truant, than white pupils from a similar social background.

Moving on to the family background variables, these have a big impact on the likelihood of truanting. Pupils with a father in a senior occupation, defined as above, are less likely to truant, with the size of the estimated effect (5–6 percentage points) being remarkably consistent across cohorts.[21] Interestingly, the marginal effect of a mother being in a senior occupation is very small and statistically insignificant in each cohort. Thus the father's occupation seems to be more important for defining the socio-economic status of a family than the mother's occupation.

Living in a privately owned home is associated with a lower incidence of truanting, the size of the effect varying between 6 and 9 percentage points across cohorts. The largest effects in Table A3.2 are reserved for the 'absence of parents' variables. As observed in the raw data above, the absence of a mother figure seems to be particularly associated with truancy, raising the probability of truanting by 10 percentage points in Cohort 10, to up to 16 percentage points in Cohort 9. Given that the average truancy rate is about 33%, these are very large effects. As well as parents, the presence of siblings can also influence truancy behaviour. The results in Table A3.2 reveal that the probability of playing truant rises by 1 percentage point with each sibling in Cohorts 8 and 9, although there is no statistically significant effect in Cohort 10.

The remaining variables in the truancy equation identify characteristics of the schools at which the respondents studied.[22] Type of school is related to truancy rates. Compared to the omitted category of comprehensive schools, pupils who attend independent schools are 8–11[23] percentage points less likely to truant. Similarly, grammar/selective school pupils are 6–7 percentage points less likely to truant than comprehensive school pupils. There is, however, no statistically significant difference in the truancy rates of comprehensive school pupils and the small number of secondary modern school pupils.

Provision of careers advice and work experience are also related to lower truancy rates. The stronger effect seems to be on the work experience variable, such that pupils who received work experience in Year 11 are 7–10 percentage points less likely to truant than pupils who did not. One interpretation of these results is that work experience maintains interest and motivation, and so makes truancy less likely. It should be acknowledged, however, that it could be a spurious relationship between the two variables. Participation in work experience is not a random occurrence but is likely to be a choice made by pupils with particular characteristics. It could then be that the same characteristics, such as motivation, ambition or ability, that make individuals more likely to participate in work experience also make them more likely to participate in school generally, ie not play truant, thus explaining the positive relationship between the two variables.

The final variables in the estimated equation were imported into the YCS data from the Local Education Authority and School Information Service (LEASIS) data set, via knowledge of the codes of the schools attended by the YCS respondents. Thus for each individual in the YCS, the imported variables tell us the proportion of pupils in his or her school that are entitled to free school meals, have special education needs but without statement, or have statemented special educational needs. The idea behind including these variables is to investigate the peer group with which the respondents mix, to see what effect that has on their truancy behaviour. In addition, a variable measuring average class size is also imported from LEASIS, to investigate whether resources spent on improving education, via smaller classes, affects truancy behaviour. The answer appears to be no, however, with the class size variable in each cohort attracting a statistically insignificant coefficient.[24] Peer groups do have an effect, though. Thus in Cohorts 8 and 9, the more pupils in an individual's school entitled to free school meals, the more likely that that pupil himself or herself will play truant. In Cohort 10, a higher proportion of special educational needs pupils in a school is associated with a higher probability of pupils in that school playing truant.

22
The standard errors in the estimated probit equation are corrected for the fact that individual respondents are clustered into schools.

23
The 11 percentage point effect in Cohort 9 is not statistically significant, due to its large standard error caused by the small number of independent schools in the sample. There are no independent schools at all in the Cohort 10 sample.

24
The class size results could also be affected by endogeneity, since the size of one's class is not a purely random event, but can be related to behaviour, if schools devote attention to problem pupils and so put disengaged pupils into smaller classes. Thus, while we would expect smaller classes to offer a more rewarding educational experience and so reduce truancy, this reverse causality of truants and disengaged pupils being put into smaller classes may be offsetting the former effect resulting in the zero effect observed in Table A3.2.

Finally, it should be noted here that attempts were made to also match into the YCS data set information on the local area in which individuals lived. The area level indicator in YCS was at best at the county level, and so data on the proportion of unemployed individuals, the proportion of senior occupation workers and the proportion of individuals qualified to NVQ Level 3 or above in each county was mapped in from Nomis (Official Labour Market Statistics). However, none of these variables had a statistically significant effect on the likelihood of playing truant, and so these results are not reported here. In addition, simply inserting regional dummy variables to identify regional differences in the estimated equations did not attract statistically significant coefficients.

The questionnaire for the survey of Cohort 10 of the YCS was changed slightly from its predecessors, and this provided some new variables of interest for the study of truancy rates. These were not included in Table A3.2, to keep the specifications the same for each cohort, and allow comparisons of the results across cohorts. Instead, the new variables were added to the Table A3.2 specification afterwards, with the results reported in Table A3.3. They show that being identified as having special educational needs, whether with statement or not, is not associated with the likelihood of truanting at all, both coefficients being highly statistically insignificant. Thus struggling with the curriculum due to educational problems does not seem to be a prime motivator of truancy behaviour. Some other variables added to the truancy equation have highly significant effects, however. They suggest that a pupil who has spent time in care (residential or foster care) is 8 percentage points more likely to truant. The impact of support from parents, where present, goes the opposite way, with pupils whose parents read to them regularly, help with homework and sorting out options, and who usually attend parents' evenings, being much less likely to play truant. The latter effect suggests that pupils whose parents usually attend parents' evenings are up to 17 percentage points less likely to truant from school. This is not simply a social class effect, with middle class parents taking more of an active role in their child's education, since the controls for social background are still in the estimated equation. Thus, at any given level of social background, the children whose parents take a strong interest in their education are much less likely to play truant. Table A3.3 also shows that the inclusion of these new variables measuring SEN, care status and parental interest does not have any effect on the relative importance or statistical significance of the other variables already in the estimated equation. It is not the case, therefore, that the impact of any variable observed above was actually working through, for example, parental interest.

In the discussion of the raw data mentioned above, a distinction was made between ever playing truant, and playing truant more seriously (ie more than occasionally). Table A3.4 therefore repeats the analysis of Table A3.2, but with serious truant behaviour, rather than any truant behaviour, as the dependent variable. As was found in the raw data, this change does not make any difference to the relative importance of the included variables' explanation of truancy behaviour. Thus, it is not the case that some groups of pupils are more likely to truant occasionally, but that they are less likely to play truant on a systematic basis. Any group of the population more likely to truant occasionally is also more likely to play truant regularly. Thus it remains the case that girls, children from families with fathers in lower-ranked occupations, children living in rented accommodation, with a father – or, particularly, a mother – missing, and who have not had careers interviews or work experience are all more likely to play truant on a regular basis. Table A3.5 also reveals that spending part of one's childhood in care, or having parents with a low interest in their education, are also still related to more truancy, when the attention shifts to serious truancy behaviour, while having SEN continues to be unrelated to the likelihood of regularly playing truant.

Key points

Investigating the factors associated with higher truancy in a multivariate setting, holding constant in each case the other factors in the equation, revealed that:

- Girls *report* a higher truancy rate than boys.

- After controlling for family background, white pupils have a higher truancy rate than other ethnic groups, although the differences are small.

- Individuals with one of their parents, especially the mother, missing, individuals with parents, particular the father, in non-professional occupations and individuals living in rented homes, are all more likely to play truant.

- Pupils in independent and grammar schools report less truancy, relative to comprehensive schools.

- If individuals receive careers advice in school, or, in particular, if they receive work experience, they are less likely to play truant.

- Whatever an individual pupil's own social background, the higher the proportion of pupils entitled to free school meals in his or her school, the more likely that individual pupil is to play truant himself/herself.

Conclusion

This chapter has looked at the topic of disengagement from the education system in the period leading up to the end of compulsory schooling, using a large, national data set. It should be pointed out that whereas a case study or interview-based research project can directly ask respondents whether they have disengaged from the education process, a study such as this one, using large, national data sets, can only use a proxy for disengagement. The advantage, of course, is that statistically significant associations in the data can be identified, rather than relying upon data from small samples chosen for qualitative research obtained using case studies or interviews.

The proxy for disengagement used in this chapter, considered the best available in existing large, national data sets, was (self-reported) truancy behaviour. Of course, it is accepted that truancy behaviour and disengagement are not exactly the same thing. For example, pupils who truant a bit during the school year, but apply themselves when exams come around and perform well, cannot really be said to have disengaged from the education process, in the usual sense of the word. Similarly, pupils who turn up for school but spend all day staring out of the window, or worse, are disruptive influences, could be said to have disengaged from education in some sense, but would not show up in truancy data. In addition, the small number of 'out of touch' pupils, as identified by Steedman and Stoney (2004), who completely drop out of the system, might not be picked up by our measures at all, if they do not bother responding to surveys such as the Youth Cohort Study. Nevertheless, to the extent that truancy and disengagement will overlap, possibly to a large extent, the analysis of truanting behaviour provides us with the best chance of using existing large, national data sets to investigate the factors associated with disengagement.

Considering first the truancy measure, whether we consider any truancy, even just the odd day, or whether we consider only more serious, systematic truancy, the same characteristics are observed as correlates. In particular, the results show that girls are more likely to report playing truant than boys. With respect to ethnic group, the differences in truancy behaviour are quite small, but the group most likely to play truant, after controlling for the effects of other variables, is that of white pupils. Family background is strongly related to truancy behaviour. Individuals with one of their parents – especially the mother – missing, individuals with parents – particular the father – in non-professional occupations, and individuals living in rented homes, are all more likely to play truant. School characteristics are similarly strongly related to truancy. The likelihood of a pupil playing truant is lower in independent and grammar schools, relative to comprehensive schools. If individuals receive careers advice in school, or if, in particular, they receive work experience, they are less likely to play truant, although the analysis cannot show whether this is due to the effects of the careers advice and work experience themselves, or whether it is just that more engaged pupils are more likely to participate in careers courses and work experience. Finally, peer effects in school can be important. The results suggest that, whatever an individual pupil's own social background, the higher the proportion of pupils entitled to free school meals in his or her school, the more likely is that individual pupil to play truant himself/herself.

Regression appendix

Table A3.1
Summary statistics for background variables
Data source: Youth Cohort Study

Variable	Cohort 8	Cohort 9	Cohort 10
Five GCSEs (A*–C)	0.592	0.574	0.642
Female	0.541	0.530	0.544
White	0.908	0.887	0.894
Black	0.015	0.018	0.021
Asian	0.062	0.069	0.073
Other ethnic group	0.015	0.015	0.012
Senior occupation father	0.361	0.336	0.371
Father's occupation missing	0.188	0.190	0.211
Senior occupation mother	0.250	0.247	0.273
Mother's occupation missing	0.254	0.229	0.209
Lives in privately owned home	0.814	0.811	0.819
Not living with father	0.164	0.164	0.184
Not living with mother	0.064	0.066	0.071
Number of siblings	1.347	1.323	1.297
North	0.078	0.059	0.053
North West	0.124	0.132	0.138
Yorkshire	0.106	0.086	0.097
East Midlands	0.076	0.077	0.083
West Midlands	0.089	0.109	0.106
South East	0.228	0.161	0.157
South West	0.098	0.097	0.099
East Anglia	0.043	0.110	0.107
Inner London	0.026	0.107	0.030
Outer London	0.072		0.072
Wales	0.060	0.061	0.058
Comprehensive school	0.810	0.855	0.786
Independent school	0.106	0.072	0.093
Secondary modern school	0.037	0.031	0.029
Grammar/selective school	0.047	0.042	0.080
Had careers class	0.906	0.864	0.853
Had own careers interview	0.850	0.914	0.899
Had work experience in Year 11	0.897	0.921	0.890
Average class size	21.64	21.58	21.83
% eligible for free school meals	0.150	0.153	0.140
% SEN with statement	0.019	0.089	0.022
% SEN without statement	0.111	0.140	0.143
Identified as having SEN			0.078
Received a statement of SEN			0.056
Previously been in residential or foster care			0.031
Parents always/frequently attended parents' evenings			0.885
Parents read to children every night or often			0.632
Frequent parental help with examination options, etc			0.587

Table A3.2
Determinants of ever playing truant
Data source: Youth Cohort Study
Robust standard errors are shown in parentheses
Regional controls included
* = Coefficient significant at 5%   ** = Coefficient significant at 1%

Variable	Cohort 8		Cohort 9		Cohort 10	
Female	0.048	(0.009)**	0.051	(0.009)**	0.042	(0.009)**
Black	0.037	(0.037)	-0.082	(0.032)*	-0.025	(0.032)
Asian	-0.001	(0.021)	-0.055	(0.020)**	-0.046	(0.020)*
Other ethnic group	0.016	(0.039)	-0.039	(0.036)	-0.025	(0.043)
Senior occupation father	-0.057	(0.010)**	-0.065	(0.011)**	-0.051	(0.011)**
Father's occupation missing	0.016	(0.014)	-0.018	(0.014)	-0.010	(0.014)
Senior occupation mother	-0.001	(0.011)	-0.008	(0.012)	-0.019	(0.011)
Mother's occupation missing	-0.037	(0.012)**	-0.019	(0.013)	-0.004	(0.012)
Live in privately owned home	-0.091	(0.013)**	-0.060	(0.013)**	-0.081	(0.013)**
Not living with father	0.103	(0.015)**	0.120	(0.014)**	0.077	(0.015)**
Not living with mother	0.132	(0.020)**	0.161	(0.022)**	0.102	(0.021)**
Number of siblings	0.012	(0.004)**	0.013	(0.004)**	0.003	(0.004)
Independent school	-0.080	(0.033)*	-0.113	(0.069)		
Secondary modern school	-0.035	(0.023)	-0.034	(0.024)	-0.033	(0.025)
Grammar/selective school	-0.066	(0.022)**	-0.064	(0.023)**	-0.066	(0.022)**
Had careers classes	-0.057	(0.018)**	-0.008	(0.014)	-0.052	(0.014)**
Had own careers interview	-0.027	(0.014)	-0.032	(0.018)	-0.037	(0.017)*
Had work experience in Year 11	-0.098	(0.023)**	-0.085	(0.024)**	-0.067	(0.021)**
Average class size	-0.004	(0.002)	-0.000	(0.002)	-0.002	(0.002)
% eligible for free school meals	0.111	(0.047)*	0.201	(0.044)**	0.039	(0.058)
% SEN with statement	0.323	(0.297)	-0.020	(0.022)	0.506	(0.299)
% SEN without statement	0.064	(0.064)	0.007	(0.045)	0.207	(0.074)**
Observations	12,612		11,203		10,848	

Table A3.3
Determinants of ever playing truant,
additional variables in Cohort 10
Data source: Youth Cohort Study
Robust standard errors are shown in parentheses
Regional controls included
* = Coefficient significant at 5% ** = Coefficient significant at 1%

Variable	Cohort 10	
Female	0.047	(0.010)**
Black	-0.048	(0.032)
Asian	-0.074	(0.020)**
Other ethnic group	-0.017	(0.045)
Identified as having SEN	-0.007	(0.023)
Received a statement of SEN	0.018	(0.027)
Previously been in residential or foster care	0.084	(0.041)*
Parents always/frequently attended parents' evenings	-0.168	(0.017)**
Parents read to children every night or often	-0.052	(0.011)**
Frequent parental help with examination options, etc	-0.064	(0.011)**
Senior occupation father	-0.038	(0.011)**
Father's occupation missing	-0.008	(0.015)
Senior occupation mother	-0.007	(0.011)
Mother's occupation missing	-0.010	(0.013)
Live in privately owned home	-0.047	(0.014)**
Not living with father	0.064	(0.015)**
Not living with mother	0.069	(0.021)**
Number of siblings	0.000	(0.004)
Secondary modern school	-0.036	(0.025)
Grammar/selective school	-0.063	(0.022)**
Had careers classes	-0.043	(0.014)**
Had own careers interview	-0.024	(0.017)
Had work experience in Year 11	-0.056	(0.021)**
Average class size	-0.003	(0.002)
% eligible for free school meals	0.052	(0.059)
% SEN with statement	0.294	(0.318)
% SEN without statement	0.184	(0.076)*
Observations	10,505	

Table A3.4
Determinants of playing truant more than occasionally
Data source: Youth Cohort Study
Robust standard errors are shown in parentheses
Regional controls included
* = Coefficient significant at 5% ** = Coefficient significant at 1%

Variable	Cohort 8		Cohort 9		Cohort 10	
Female	0.013	(0.005)*	0.022	(0.005)**	0.007	(0.005)
Black	0.008	(0.020)	-0.036	(0.013)**	-0.015	(0.014)
Asian	-0.016	(0.011)	-0.019	(0.010)	-0.017	(0.009)
Other ethnic group	-0.003	(0.022)	-0.005	(0.019)	-0.021	(0.020)
Senior occupation father	-0.028	(0.006)**	-0.030	(0.006)**	-0.021	(0.006)**
Father's occupation missing	0.014	(0.008)	-0.004	(0.007)	-0.008	(0.007)
Senior occupation mother	-0.021	(0.006)**	-0.003	(0.007)	-0.002	(0.006)
Mother's occupation missing	-0.004	(0.006)	-0.003	(0.007)	0.010	(0.007)
Live in privately owned home	-0.067	(0.008)**	-0.043	(0.008)**	-0.044	(0.008)**
Not living with father	0.028	(0.009)**	0.046	(0.009)**	0.037	(0.008)**
Not living with mother	0.081	(0.014)**	0.105	(0.016)**	0.037	(0.012)**
Number of siblings	0.005	(0.002)*	0.003	(0.002)	0.001	(0.002)
Independent school	-0.004	(0.048)	-0.023	(0.031)		
Secondary modern school	0.004	(0.014)	-0.013	(0.012)	-0.005	(0.013)
Grammar/selective school	-0.014	(0.013)	-0.049	(0.009)**	-0.030	(0.011)**
Had careers classes	-0.056	(0.012)**	-0.022	(0.008)**	-0.018	(0.008)*
Had own careers interview	-0.030	(0.009)**	-0.051	(0.012)**	-0.058	(0.011)**
Had work experience in Year 11	-0.070	(0.015)**	-0.073	(0.015)**	-0.058	(0.013)**
Average class size	0.001	(0.001)	0.000	(0.001)	0.002	(0.001)*
% eligible for free school meals	0.040	(0.025)	0.093	(0.023)**	0.048	(0.028)
% SEN with statement	0.197	(0.148)	-0.002	(0.011)	0.178	(0.134)
% SEN without statement	0.052	(0.034)	0.023	(0.022)	0.123	(0.034)**
Observations	12,612		11,203		10,848	

Table A3.5
Determinants of playing truant more than occasionally,
additional variables in Cohort 10
Data source: Youth Cohort Study
Robust standard errors are shown in parentheses
Regional controls included
* = Coefficient significant at 5% ** = Coefficient significant at 1%

Variable	Cohort 10	
Female	0.007	(0.005)
Black	−0.024	(0.012)*
Asian	−0.022	(0.008)**
Other ethnic group	−0.014	(0.021)
Identified as having SEN	0.004	(0.012)
Received a statement of SEN	0.026	(0.017)
Previously been in residential or foster care	0.054	(0.025)*
Parents always/frequently attended parents' evenings	−0.077	(0.010)**
Parents read to children every night or often	−0.008	(0.006)
Frequent parental help with examination options, etc	−0.017	(0.005)**
Senior occupation father	−0.018	(0.006)**
Father's occupation missing	−0.008	(0.006)
Senior occupation mother	0.002	(0.006)
Mother's occupation missing	0.006	(0.007)
Live in privately owned home	−0.029	(0.008)**
Not living with father	0.030	(0.008)**
Not living with mother	0.022	(0.011)*
Number of siblings	−0.000	(0.002)
Secondary modern school	−0.003	(0.013)
Grammar/selective school	−0.025	(0.011)*
Had careers classes	−0.014	(0.007)
Had own careers interview	−0.052	(0.011)**
Had work experience in Year 11	−0.047	(0.013)**
Average class size	0.002	(0.001)
% eligible for free school meals	0.055	(0.027)*
% SEN with statement	0.111	(0.131)
% SEN without statement	0.103	(0.033)**
Observations	10,505	

4 The initial post-compulsory education experiences of former school truants

Introduction

The previous two chapters in this report have essentially been scene-setting, describing firstly the characteristics of individuals who under-achieve, and then the characteristics of individuals who truant, taken as an indicator (though not a perfect representation) of disengagement.

This chapter starts to put the two concepts together, and in particular look at the relationship between them. It will aim to show that school performance, in particular performance in GCSE exams at the end of post-compulsory education at the age of 16 is lower, on average, among those who have truanted.

A lack of good GCSEs can prevent, or at least dissuade, pupils from continuing in learning in an academic setting, such as pursuing A-levels. Of course, it certainly need not prevent or even dissuade such individuals who have failed to achieve good GCSEs from learning altogether, and so the analysis continues by considering who, among the group of low-achieving former truants, nevertheless continues (or re-engages) in learning by participating in further education. By gaining an understanding of the types of former disengaged individuals who participate in further education, it may be possible to understand why they do this, which could help in deciding how to increase participation in the future.

Before beginning the analysis, it may be helpful to reiterate the provisos described in this report. First, it is not being claimed that disengagement is the only source of under-achievement. Individuals could remain fully engaged in the education process, but still not achieve their potential, for example because of some change in their circumstances, inability to cope with formal exams, or many other reasons. In fact, there need be no causal link from disengagement to under-achievement, but perhaps the reverse, with failure in exams leading individuals to lose confidence and withdraw from full participation in education. Similarly, there may be no causal relationship at all between disengagement and under-achievement, but both may be the outcomes of other variables, such as low ability, special needs, problems at home, psychological problems etc. All this research will aim to show, therefore, is the association between truancy (as the chosen measure of disengagement) and low achievement, and then look at the outcomes for individuals identified with disengagement and low achievement.

The second point to be made is that it is not being argued that truancy is the only manifestation of disengagement, nor that truancy necessarily reflects disengagement. For example, a pupil who continues to attend school all of the time, but daydreams constantly through classes and submits no work could be thought of as having disengaged from the education process, but of course would not show up in truancy statistics. Similarly, a young person who occasionally misses school to attend to some caring duties, looking after a sick or disabled parent or sibling, for example, but does their utmost to catch up on the school work missed, should not be thought of as having disengaged from the education process, but would nevertheless show up in truancy data. More simply, pupils could truant at certain, more relaxed parts of the school calendar, but still exert plenty of effort when exam time comes around, and so again should not be thought of as disengaged.

The use of the truancy variable is simply out of necessity, as it seemed to be the variable most closely related to disengagement available in large, national data sets. Its appropriateness can in some ways be judged by the results that it produces. If the final results are plausible, given that truancy is supposed to be indicating disengagement, then this would provide the truancy variable with some validity. Ultimately, however, it must be borne in mind that the results refer to self-reported truancy, and not a more direct measure of disengagement.

The next section looks at some recent literature on disengaged school learners and further education, while the subsequent sections contain the results of the analyses and the conclusions.

Literature review

As before, this section is not intended to be a complete review of all research undertaken on this subject, but simply an outline of recent relevant evidence published since Steedman and Stoney (2004) undertook their review of evidence on disengagement.

A study by Alderson and Arnold (1999) found that school students have low expectations of being treated fairly at school. Although the students agreed that there are important rules that need to be kept, they considered teachers to be unbending about minor, petty regulations. They felt strongly that they would like to be respected and listened to by adults, but said that they were not. It is therefore pertinent that this review of recent literature into the factors influencing participation in post-16 learning among the disengaged and disaffected was unable to find a single study that reports the views of this population.

A study by Bricheno and Younger (2004) of school students' views about their preferred learning styles offers some clues. It finds that both boys and girls overwhelmingly prefer practical work and activity-based working, for example practical science. The same findings are reported in a Scottish study by Kendal *et al.* (2001), which tried to find out how to re-engage disaffected students. It also found that there has to be a major change in teaching style and content. Active learning is effective, as is offering praise, reassurance and constructive feedback. The content of the learning needs to match students' perceptions of their needs, and appear relevant and meaningful. Deakin Crick *et al.* (2005) also found that at schools, strategies need to be in place encouraging engagement with learning by relating learning to students' experience. Both Deakin Crick *et al.* and Kendal *et al.* report that for learning to take place, effective relationships need to be established between teachers and students. This style of teaching, according to Deakin Crick *et al.* involves dialogue and negotiation rather than traditional, authoritarian methods of control.

Helpful though these findings are, they fail to report how extensive the disaffection is: are students disaffected with learning, or more broadly with society? As long as schools are expected to not only teach, but also inculcate students in the acceptable mores and expected behaviour of society, it is apparent that these two roles will often be in competition. Moreover, it is probable that much disillusion with learning springs from the contradiction inherent in this dual role.

Morris (2004) sees effective advice and guidance as one way of encouraging disaffected students to overcome barriers to learning and raise aspirations. However, she also found that the present structures in schools militate against this, with advice being biased and a tendency to pigeon-hole students. It is claimed that it is important to give advice and guidance early (Watson 2004). This might be true. However, as Morris (2004) points out, the disengaged learners will need advice once the results of their GCSE examinations are known, yet at this point the onus is on the individual to seek it.

To make matters worse, the very structure of post-16 education seems to make it easy to advise achieving students and difficult to advise the others, for the progression route for the former is simple and well known – A-levels – while the route for the latter is very complex, with all sorts of different qualifications that might be studied, often in bundles (Foskett 2004; Morris 2004; Watson 2004). For example, as Watson points out, a student who signs up for a Level 2 qualification might also enrol for three other, compulsory key skills qualifications. Watson found that not only is this structure difficult to understand, it is difficult to negotiate successfully. It is clear therefore, that if there is to be further participation in learning post-16 by the disengaged and disaffected, these pathways and qualifications will need to be made much simpler.

A study by Wiseman (2004) reports the kinds of support that providers of post-16 learning can offer to influence further participation. While these findings are helpful, they fail to explain what providers should be doing to recruit the disengaged in the first place. Wiseman claims that the factors influencing participation are complex and inter-related. Strategies have to be combined and implemented in full; none will work in isolation.

For FE providers, Wiseman identifies four kinds of support that are required:

- pre-course, which should ensure that potential learners make the most appropriate choices

- on-course, which should include flexible delivery that takes account of student needs, student-centred assessment strategies and clear teaching objectives

- academic support, which is essential to those who have been away from learning, and this involves providing additional feedback and taking remedial action as required

- pastoral support, which is crucial for 'at-risk' students.

For work-based providers, it is also necessary to combine a number of factors. These include:

- improving the availability of times when training is offered

- making retention a priority in all aspects of recruitment, assignments and assessments

- improving the frequency and quality of contact by providers with learners

- improving the integration of key skills learning

- improving staff recruitment, retention and development

- improving the commitment of employers to work-based learning.

Farlie (2004 makes similar points about the necessary stages for effective work-based learning, which he calls 'the learning cycle'.

Two studies report relevant interventions. One, by Webb and Vulliamy (2004) is of a three-year DfES-funded project which encouraged a multi-agency approach to helping school students at risk of exclusion. Five social workers were based in schools and worked closely with students and their families. Although the aim of the project was to reduce exclusions from school, where it was successful it also helped re-engage students in learning. All the same, the project uncovered a range of cultural differences between social workers and school staff which would need to be ironed out for this programme to be repeated. Despite this, it appears that by establishing this programme there is a tacit acknowledgement that teaching and learning on the one hand, and the process of social care and support on the other, need different kinds of interventions if one is not to get in the way of the other.

The other intervention study by Golden *et al.* (2005) evaluated the first two years of the Increased Flexibility Programme (IFP) for 14–16 year olds. This was introduced in 2002 by the DfES in order to 'create enhanced vocational and work-related learning opportunities for 14–16 year olds who can benefit most'. Further education colleges, training providers, employers and schools formed partnerships to offer two-year vocational courses leading to vocational qualifications. Although the report does not state how students were chosen for this programme, it is implied that they would be those who were disengaged and with low levels of achievement.

In general, the broader curriculum had benefits for students and made them more likely to achieve qualifications. It is also claimed that it helped them achieve 'softer' outcomes, such as improved social and communication skills and more positive attitudes towards school (and hence, one presumes, to learning). Moreover, it helped a majority (56%) to decide what to do next. However, the study had no comparison group of any kind and therefore its findings can only be considered indicative.

Finally, an important finding in a study by Rennison *et al.* (2005) is that any participation is better than none, because the longer somebody is not in education or training, the less likely it is they ever will be. More needs to be found out about this particular population, in order to devise effective strategies to help them engage with further education.

Much of the work in this area of re-engagement has therefore been case study work looking at 'what works' in terms of re-engaging or sustaining engagement of pupils. As such, the analysis to be presented here does not directly add to this literature, since the discussion here will be on *who* re-engages rather than *why*. It is to this new analysis of disengagement and re-engagement in further education that the chapter now turns.

Data sets and the variables

The Youth Cohort Study

The data for this chapter again comes from the Youth Cohort Study (YCS), specifically Cohorts 8, 9 and 10, as were used in the previous chapter. Again, the reason for using three separate cohorts is to see whether results are replicated across studies, which would give them more weight. The three cohorts were interviewed in 1996, 1998 and 2000 respectively, which in each case was in the spring following their completion of post-compulsory schooling, meaning that they were 16 or 17 years old when first interviewed. Later in the chapter, when we are considering outcomes of learning in further education, we will make use of surveys undertaken by the respondents two years after their initial interview, which is the second time they were contacted in the case of Cohort 8, and the third time in the case of Cohorts 9 and 10.

The truancy variable

To reiterate the discussion in the previous chapter, the key variable used in the analysis to be presented here is derived from a question asking respondents to self-report their levels of truancy. The question asks (with the percentage responding with each answer in the three cohorts as shown):

Thinking back to Year 11 (fifth year), did you play truant from school:

	Cohort 8	Cohort 9	Cohort 10
1 for weeks at a time	1.8%	1.7%	1.3%
2 for several days at a time	1.8%	2.0%	1.5%
3 for particular days or lessons	5.7%	5.5%	4.9%
4 for the odd day or lesson	26.7%	25.7%	24.2%
5 never?	64.1%	65.2%	68.1%

Data source: Youth Cohort Study

As before, two different groups of truants are identified from this question and used in the analysis that follows, namely all those who ever truanted (categories 1–4 above), and those more serious truants who have been absent for more than just the odd day or lesson (categories 1–3 above). The serious truants are therefore a subset of all truants. It can be seen from the percentages in the above table that around two-thirds of respondents claim never to have truanted. Of the truants, the majority claim to have played truant for only the odd day or lesson. Our definition of serious truants omits these groups, and so the serious truants identified below represent just less than 10% of the sample.

Outcome variables

The first outcome that we want to consider is GCSE results, to determine what impact truancy in Year 11 has on academic performance. Although there is detailed information in the YCS on exam outcomes, including the subject studied and grade awarded for every one, it was decided to simply focus on whether or not individuals achieve five or more GCSEs at Grade C or above, because of the attention focused on this outcome measure, and to avoid having to present a confusing array of results all related to GCSE performance. The acquisition of five GCSEs, whatever the grade, is also considered, however, as in the previous chapter.

GCSEs mark the end of compulsory education, and the next outcome to be considered is what individuals then choose to do. Again, the YCS has good information on economic activity at the time of the survey, allowing us to identify whether respondents have continued in education, found a job, enlisted on a government training scheme or are not in education, employment or training (NEET).

The remainder of this chapter, and most of the next, focus on vocational qualifications and what role they play for those disengaged at school. This chapter will look at who participates in vocational education, and the consequences for those who do. Chapter 5 will then look at the impact such participation in vocational education has on labour market outcomes.

Other variables

The same control or explanatory variables found in the YCS and used in the previous chapter will be used again here, in particular gender, ethnicity, family status (parental occupation and ownership of home), family composition (presence of both parents in family home and number of siblings), region of residence, indicators of school quality (school type, average class size, proportions of pupil roll with special educational needs (SEN) or entitled to free school meals, provision of careers advice and work experience), respondents' own SEN status, whether they have ever been in social care and the extent of parental interest in their education. Table A3.1 in the previous chapter provided some basic descriptive statistics for these variables.

Results

GCSE achievement

As discussed above, the first analysis involves looking at GCSE outcomes for all students and identifying which individuals achieve five or more GCSEs, focusing in particular on the achievements of truants relative to non-truants.[25] This allows us to see whether the truancy variable used has real information and has real effects, and to examine to what extent it can be thought of as an indicator of disengagement.

Across the full samples, between 57 and 64% of individuals achieve five or more good GCSEs, according to cohort. We want to know how this proportion varies according to truancy behaviour. The answer is provided in Table 4.1 and Figure 4.1.

[25]
Note that, given the nature of the YCS data, we can only use an absolute measure of performance, for example whether individuals achieve five or more good GCSEs in this analysis, and cannot create the more refined measure of under-achievement that was used in Chapter 2 above, taking account of the individual's own earlier test scores.

Table 4.1
Percentage acquiring five or more good GCSEs, by cohort and level of truancy
Data source: Youth Cohort Study

	Cohort 8	Cohort 9	Cohort 10
No truancy	67.1	65.0	70.6
Any who play truant	44.8	42.9	50.1
Serious truants only	25.4	23.6	25.2

Figure 4.1
Percentage acquiring five or more good GCSEs, by cohort and level of truancy
Data source: Youth Cohort Study

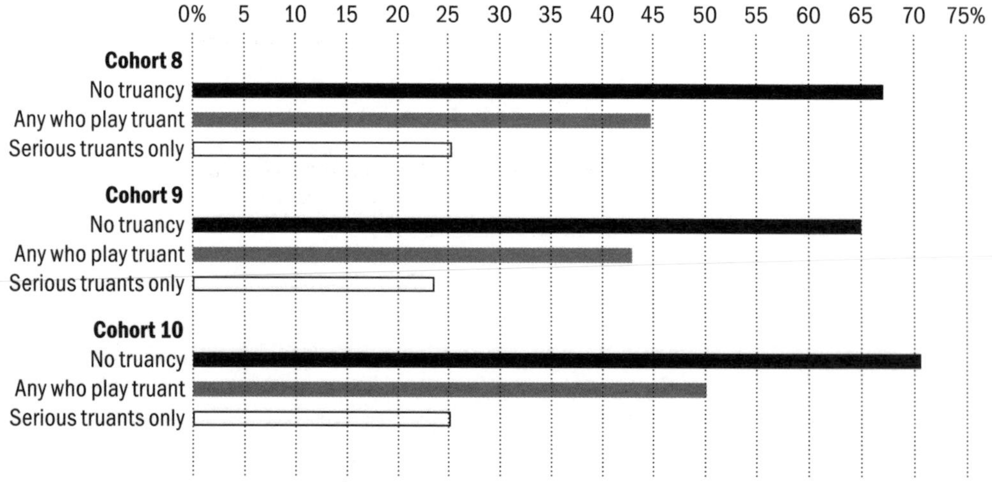

Table 4.1 and Figure 4.1 reveal very similar differences in GCSE attainment between truancy groups in each of the three cohorts. Among those who never play truant, just over two-thirds acquire five or more good GCSEs at the end of Year 11. Among those who played truant at least once during Year 11, about half (in Cohort 10) or just less than half (in Cohorts 8 and 9) achieve this level of success in their GCSEs. Focusing only on the serious truants, who have missed significant numbers of classes, GCSE success falls significantly again, with only around one-quarter of this group reaching the 'five or more' benchmark.

As discussed in Chapter 2, an argument can be made for looking at a benchmark of five GCSEs at any grade, rather than only at Grade C or above, since a failure to reach five Grade A*–C GCSEs could reflect many factors, including a lack of natural ability, whereas a failure to even acquire five GCSEs at Grade G could be more indicative of disengagement from the education process. The problem with this definition, as was found in Chapter 2, is that most pupils (in the YCS, 91–93% according to cohort) manage to reach this benchmark, and so the analysis is restricted to a small number of individuals.

Table 4.2 and Figure 4.2 show how the success rate of five or more Grade A*–G GCSEs varies across truancy categories.

Table 4.2
Percentage acquiring five or more GCSEs at any grade,
by cohort and level of truancy
Data source: Youth Cohort Study

	Cohort 8	Cohort 9	Cohort 10
No truancy	95.9	94.5	95.8
Any who play truant	87.1	86.1	89.3
Serious truants only	70.1	72.0	76.2

Figure 4.2
Percentage acquiring five or more GCSEs at any grade,
by cohort and level of truancy
Data source: Youth Cohort Study

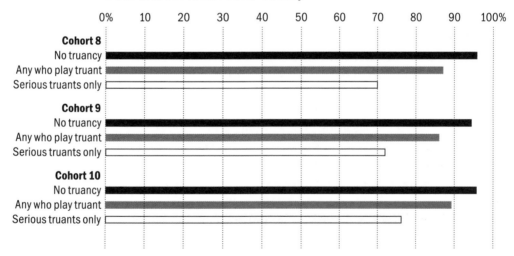

Thus almost all (95%) pupils who do not truant in Year 11 manage to acquire five GCSEs at any grade. Even among those who have truanted, almost 90% achieve this level, showing that those who truant and fail to acquire at least five GCSEs (labelled very low-achieving former truants below) are quite a special group. For the most part, for the analyses that follow, therefore, a benchmark of five or more Grades A*–C will be used when defining achievement levels. Among the serious truants only, 70–76% obtain five GCSEs at least at Grade G.

It should be noted that such correlations between variables do not prove causation, so that it is not necessarily the case that the low achievement has been caused by the truancy. There could be many other factors that have influenced both the propensity to play truant and low achievement in GCSE exams, thus leading to an apparent relationship between the two.

In Table A4.1, therefore, we move to a multivariate setting,[26] controlling for as many other possible influences on GCSE scores as the data allows. By holding these other factors constant, we get a clearer picture of the direct effect, if any, of truancy on achievement.

It is still the case, however, that there probably remain unobserved, and therefore uncontrolled for, characteristics of individuals, such as motivation, natural ability and interest in learning, that could influence both truancy and achievement, and so it cannot be claimed that these results prove a causal relationship.

The results in the first row of Table A4.1 show that, with a remarkable consistency across cohorts, those who have played truant in Year 11 are about 20 percentage points less likely to achieve five or more GCSEs at Grade C or above, compared to individuals who did not truant at all. This difference is almost equal to the difference in achievement rates observed between the two groups in the raw data in Table 4.1. It therefore appears that none of this difference in raw achievement rates between truants and non-truants can be explained by differences in the two groups' characteristics, such as gender, ethnicity, socio-economic status of family, family composition, nor by differences in the characteristics of the schools attended by the two groups.

Looking at the coefficients on the other variables, these suggest that young women are more likely than young men to acquire five or more good GCSEs, by a considerable margin (10 percentage points). Considering ethnicity, there seems to be little difference in achievement between black and white pupils, after controlling for other variables in the estimated equation, while Asian pupils are 11–14 percentage points more likely to acquire five or more good GCSEs than both.

As expected, GCSE achievement is strongly related to the socio-economic status of pupils' families. Having a father or mother in a senior occupation[27] has a strong, independent effect on performance (suggesting of course that performance will be highest among pupils who have both parents in senior occupations). Pupils living in a privately owned home are around 17–20 percentage points more likely to reach the five or more good GCSE benchmark than pupils living in rented accommodation.

Smaller effects are observed on family composition. The absence of a father[28] does not seem to have any effect on GCSE performance, although pupils living in a home without their mothers are 5–9 percentage points less likely to achieve good GCSEs. Number of siblings has a small, but statistically significant, impact, with the probability of acquiring five or more good GCSEs falling by 2 percentage points, on average, for each extra sibling.

As expected, GCSE results also vary by school characteristics. Relative to comprehensive schools, which form the reference category for school type, there is evidence that independent schools have a higher achievement rate in Cohort 8, though a lack of independent schools in Cohort 9, and their absence completely in Cohort 10, means there is no supporting evidence from other cohorts. Pupils attending a grammar or selective schools have a 31–37 percentage point higher chance of obtaining five or more good GCSEs, while those attending secondary modern schools have a 10–13 percentage point lower probability of acquiring such qualifications, again relative to comprehensive schools and holding other characteristics constant.

26
Since the dependent variable is a dichotomous variable indicating the achievement or otherwise of five or more good GCSEs, the estimation procedure used is a probit equation, as described in previous chapters. In all the tables of results, marginal effects for all the variables are shown, rather than their raw coefficients.

27
Defined as the top three categories in the Standard Occupational Classification, ie manager, professional or associate professional.

28
Strictly speaking, the absence of a father in the home at the time of the interview, rather than during the respondent's GCSE year.

Independent of school type, the larger the proportion of pupils eligible for free school meals, and the larger the proportion with special educational needs, (though not for Cohort 9 in the latter case) the lower the probability of any particular pupil at those schools obtaining five or more good GCSEs, thus illustrating the importance of peer effects. There are no statistically significant negative effects of average class sizes on GCSE performance in any cohort, which might have been expected, given the supposed benefits of smaller classes. However, this result is consistent with much research in the literature that fails to observe higher pupil achievement in smaller classes. The problem is that class size can be a choice variable, and although smaller classes should have educational benefits, schools may choose to put poorer performing pupils into smaller classes, in order that they receive more individual attention, thus leading to small classes being associated with lower performance, and thus offsetting the benefits of small classes on performance in any empirical estimation of the relationship between the two variables. Research that has attempted to control for the endogenous nature of class size has been more successful in finding negative, though small, effects of class size on pupil performance.

Turning to experience within schools, the results indicate that pupils who have had careers advice or work experience have a higher probability of obtaining five or more good GCSEs. Again, however, it is unclear whether this is a true causal relationship. While there may be beneficial effects of such experiences on GCSE performance, for example, through increasing motivation or enthusiasm, it could also be the case that both participation in the careers service or work experience, and GCSE performance, are all just outcomes of individuals' drive for success, aptitude or involvement in school processes. This suggests that the pupils who are going to do well in their GCSEs are more likely to be the ones taking advantage of careers advice or work experience.

As in all analyses using the YCS data in this report (and those using the data from the Labour Force Survey in the following chapter), dummy variables for broad statistical regions were included among the explanatory variables, but not reported in results tables due to the regional differences being statistically insignificant. In the GCSE achievement equations, however, one regional result did stand out, and that was a higher achievement rate, holding constant the other characteristics in the equation, in London compared to the rest of the country.

Finally, in the last column of Table A4.1, the equation for Cohort 10 is re-estimated to include some additional variables based on questions that were new to the Cohort 10 survey. The results for these variables show that individuals with special educational needs are much less likely to achieve five or more good GCSEs. The coefficient on the variable indicating individuals who have spent at least some of their childhood in residential or foster care is negative, suggesting a lower probability of GCSE success, although the finding is not statistically significant. Finally, three variables are included to measure parents' interest or involvement in their children's education. The strongest result shows that individuals whose parents regularly attended parents' evenings are 16 percentage points more likely to achieve five or more good GCSEs, even after controlling for the other variables in the equation, which include measures of social class.

The results also show a smaller positive effect of parents reading to their children when young on eventual GCSE success, although there is a surprising negative coefficient on the variable indicating parents who help their children with homework, choosing options etc. The likely cause may be that the three variables are all picking up aspects of parents' interest, and cannot successfully identify their separate effects. If each of the three parents' interest variables, including the helping with homework/options one, are included in the estimated equation on their own, or as one composite variable, they attract a large, positive, statistically significant coefficient.

Table A4.2 looks at the variables associated with obtaining five GCSEs at any grade. Although the size of the effects are generally much smaller than in Table A4.1 – which is to be expected, given that most pupils obtain at least five GCSEs at any grade and so there is less variation in the dependent variable across observations to be explained – the pattern of statistical significance across the categories of the various explanatory variables remains the same. As for truancy, those who truant are 3–5 percentage points less likely to reach this benchmark of at least five GCSEs at any grade.

In Table A4.3, the same equations are estimated as in Table A4.1, only the indicator of truancy behaviour changes from all who committed any sort of truancy in Year 11 to only those who indicated playing more serious truant, ie missing weeks or several days at a time, or regularly missing particular days or lessons. Not surprisingly, the results reveal that this group of truants are even less likely to achieve five or more GCSEs at Grade C or above than the group of all truants, with the marginal effects showing that serious truants are 29–36 percentage points less likely to acquire five or more good GCSEs than non-serious truants.

The effects of the remaining variables in Table A4.3 following the change in truancy variable are barely changed from those in Table A4.1, and so will not be discussed again.

Table A4.4 considers the impact of serious truancy on the likelihood of obtaining five or more GCSEs at any grade. As before, the impact is reduced relative to the Grade A*–C measure, but is still large, an 8–13 percentage point lower probability of obtaining five GCSEs at any grade, and highly statistically significant.

Key points

■ Individuals who truanted in Year 11 at school are less likely to acquire five or more Grade A*–C GCSEs, or five or more Grade A*–G GCSEs.

■ This effect remains after controlling for background characteristics.

■ The coefficients on the background characteristics suggest a higher likelihood of success for females, Asian pupils, those from good socio-economic backgrounds, those living with their mother, those who attended independent or grammar schools, those with fewer pupils with SEN or entitled to free school meals, those who had careers advice or work experience in Year 11, those without SEN themselves and those with supportive parents.

What individuals do next

So far, this chapter has focused on the impact of truancy on GCSE success. The main aim of this chapter, however, is to see to what extent formerly disengaged pupils manage to re-engage in further education through post-compulsory study, and so what follows is an examination of what YCS respondents say they are doing at the time of their Sweep 1 survey, in the spring following their completion of compulsory education.

First, however, the indicator of disengaged pupils will be changed from those who have played truant to those who have played truant *and* failed to achieve five or more good GCSEs. As discussed earlier, not all truants have necessarily disengaged from the education process. They may have been taking time off school to care for a relative, while keeping up their studies at home, or they may have truanted in the early part of a school year, but re-engaged with their education at exam time. If individuals achieve their five or more good GCSEs, they are not regarded as disengaged. From this point on, therefore, the indicator of disengagement will be low-achieving (in terms of fewer than five good GCSEs) former truants, or low-achieving former serious truants, with the reference category being all others (ie those who never truanted, plus those who did, but still managed to achieve the five Grade A*–C GCSE benchmark). At various points, very low-achieving former truants (those who truanted and failed to obtain five GCSEs even at Grade G) will also be considered.

Table 4.3 and Figure 4.3 show the economic activity of the three groups (low-achieving former truants, low-achieving former serious truants and others, using the five or more Grade A*–C GCSE measure) at the time of their Sweep 1 survey, for each cohort separately.

Table 4.3
Percentage in each economic activity at age 16 or 17,
by truancy category and cohort
Data source: Youth Cohort Study

	Low-achieving truants	Low-achieving serious truants	All others
Cohort 8			
Full-time education	49.3	34.1	85.6
Full-time job	15.7	19.6	4.7
Part-time job	3.3	4.5	1.3
Government training	16.2	17.4	5.6
Unemployed	12.3	19.0	1.9
Something else	3.2	5.4	0.9
Cohort 9			
Full-time education	42.5	29.4	82.8
Full-time job	19.3	24.5	5.4
Part-time job	5.3	6.1	1.6
Government training	17.8	17.3	7.6
Unemployed	12.3	18.7	2.2
Something else	2.8	4.1	0.6
Cohort 10			
Full-time education	44.8	34.1	84.4
Full-time job	16.6	21.5	4.7
Part-time job	5.0	6.1	1.4
Government training	16.6	14.4	6.7
Unemployed	13.4	18.2	1.8
Something else	3.7	5.7	1.0

Figure 4.3
Percentage in each economic activity at age 16 or 17,
by truancy category and cohort
Data source: Youth Cohort Study
■ = Low-achieving truants
■ = Low-achieving serious truants
□ = All others

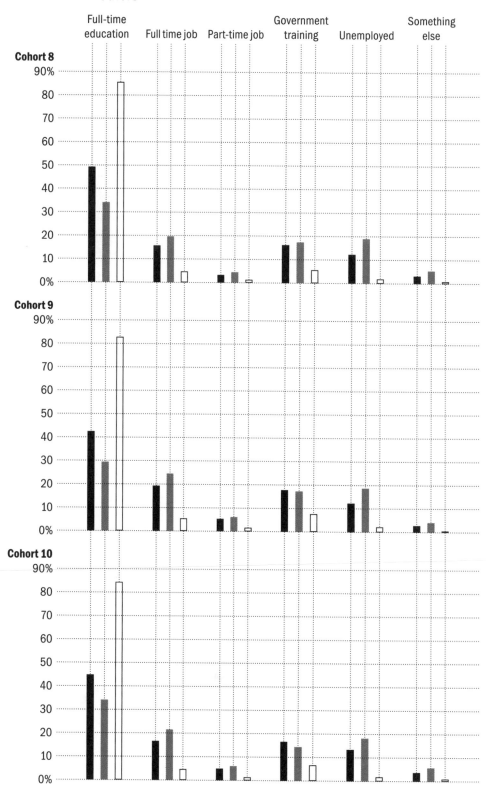

The pattern of results is very similar across the three cohorts. Thus among the non-disengaged group (never played truant, or did play truant but still obtained five or more good GCSEs), the vast majority (83–86%) are still in full-time education at the time of their first YCS survey. Most of the remainder are either in work or government training, with very few NEET.

Looking at those who have truanted and failed to achieve five good GCSEs, the picture is very different. Looking first at the 'any truancy' group, less than half (43–49%) are in full-time education in the year following compulsory schooling. Of those not in education, most are in employment or government training. However, there are significant numbers (15–17%) outside the labour market (unemployed or doing 'something else'). Among low-achieving former serious truants, the pattern changes again (suggesting that the truancy variable contains real information about the attitudes and likely outcomes of individuals, since the only difference between this group and the former group is the extent of their truancy). Thus, only around one-third (29–34%) of the serious truant low-achievers are still in full-time education. The lower numbers in education compared to the 'any truant' group emerge in higher numbers in both employment and unemployment. Just less than one-quarter of this group in each cohort are NEET.

Table 4.4 and Figure 4.4 perform the same analysis of economic activity, but using the five Grade A*–G GCSE rather than the five A*–C GCSE benchmark for low achievement.

Table 4.4
percentage in each economic activity at age 16 or 17,
by truancy category and cohort
Data source: Youth Cohort Study

	Very low-achieving truants	Very low-achieving serious truants	All others
Cohort 8			
Full-time education	20.8	16.3	81.0
Full-time job	22.5	23.5	6.1
Part-time job	5.8	6.2	1.5
Government training	17.6	15.5	7.2
Unemployed	26.8	31.3	3.0
Something else	6.4	7.2	1.2
Cohort 9			
Full-time education	20.1	14.1	77.6
Full-time job	25.4	27.6	7.7
Part-time job	6.1	6.0	2.1
Government training	18.5	16.8	8.5
Unemployed	23.3	27.6	3.2
Something else	6.6	7.9	0.9
Cohort 10			
Full-time education	23.6	20.1	80.2
Full-time job	19.9	20.5	6.7
Part-time job	6.0	5.3	1.9
Government training	16.3	12.7	7.2
Unemployed	25.8	30.7	2.9
Something else	8.4	10.7	1.1

Figure 4.4
percentage in each economic activity at age 16 or 17,
by truancy category and cohort
Data source: Youth Cohort Study
■ = Very low-achieving truants
■ = Very low-achieving serious truants
□ = All others

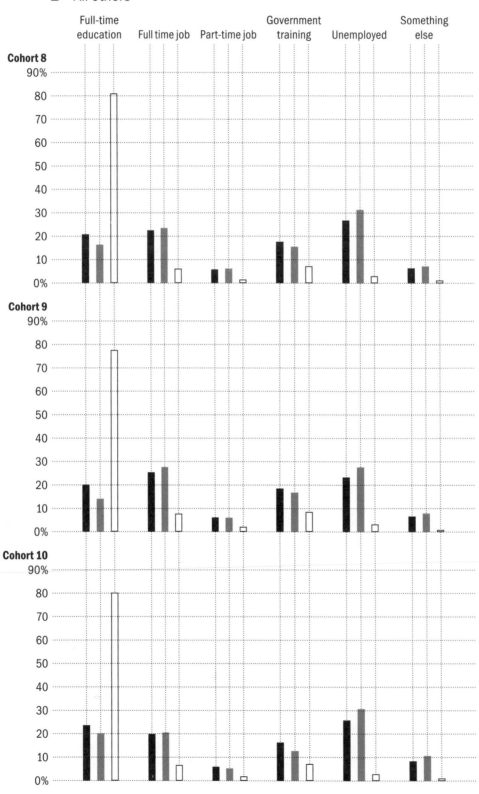

As expected, the economic position of those former truants who have not acquired five GCSEs at *any* grade is considerably worse, on average, than those who failed to reach five Grade A*–C GCSEs. Among these very low-achieving former truants, only 20–24% are still in full-time education in the year following the end of compulsory schooling, which is a big fall relative to the *low-achieving* truants. This fall in the education participation rate is offset only to some extent by higher employment rates, and barely at all by higher training rates, meaning that a much higher proportion of these very low-achieving former truants are unemployed (23–27%) or inactive (6–8%), even at this young age.

Among those individuals who played serious truant at school and failed to get five GCSEs at any grade, the full-time education participation rate falls to just 14–20%. Clearly, only limited numbers of this group are re-engaging. About one-quarter to one-third are in employment, but around 30% are unemployed and a further 10% inactive.

Key points

In the year after the completion of compulsory education, those who truanted and failed to achieve five or more good GCSEs at school are:

- less likely to still be in full-time education
- more likely to be in a job
- more likely to be in government training
- much more likely to be unemployed
- more likely to be outside the labour market altogether.

If they truanted and failed to obtain five GCSEs at *any* grade, their economic position is even worse on average, with lower education participation rates and higher unemployment and inactivity rates.

The factors associated with staying in full-time education

The previous section showed that, while low-achieving former truants are less likely to continue in full-time education, a significant minority do in fact re-engage (if indeed disengagement was the reason for their truancy and low achievement), and participate in post-compulsory education. However, this is in part related to the extent of their low achievement, with the very low achievers being less likely to participate. The aim of this section is to see whether there are particular characteristics of individuals, their families or their schools, associated with such continuation in education, to try to better understand why some previous truants stay on and others do not.

The results of a multivariate probit equation with a dummy variable indicating being in full-time education as the dependent variable – for a sample containing all who truanted in Year 11 and failed to achieve five good GCSEs – are shown in Table A4.5. The first row shows that, among those who disengaged during compulsory schooling according to the definition being used here, girls were significantly more likely to re-engage and participate in post-compulsory full-time education than boys, with the probability difference by gender being 7–9 percentage points across different cohorts.

The coefficients on the ethnicity variables are particularly striking, and show that, relative to the omitted category of white pupils, those from other ethnic groups are far more likely to be in full-time education, controlling for other factors in the equation. The difference in this likelihood is 23–32 percentage points between black pupils and white pupils, 30–39 percentage points between Asian pupils and white pupils, and 22–37 percentage points between other ethnic groups and white pupils. This range of impacts across cohorts is wider than the range of gender effects, due to the small numbers in the ethnic minority categories, making the estimates less stable. The size of the ethnicity effects is therefore difficult to estimate with any precision, but the results strongly suggest that there is some statistically significant ethnicity effect. Putting the gender and ethnicity results together suggests that it is white boys who, having disengaged from the education process, are the least likely to re-engage in post-compulsory education.[29]

29
Recall that exactly the same effect was noticed in Chapter 2. Among those who under-achieved at Key stage 3, the least likely to nevertheless get their studies back on track and achieve the GCSE results that their Key stage 2 results predicted they should were white boys.

Other results in Table A4.5 show that family background continues to play an important role in determining whether former truants participate in full-time education. Thus, individuals whose parents are employed in senior occupations, and those who live in privately owned homes, are significantly more likely to get back on track by studying post-school. The absence of a father in the individual's home does not have any impact at all on whether they participate in full-time post-compulsory education, but those who do not live with their mother are significantly less likely to be studying, by 12–17 percentage points compared to those with a maternal figure at home. The number of siblings an individual has does not seem to have any effect on participation either way.

The final set of variables relates to characteristics of the individuals' schools. There does not seem to be any positive effect associated with grammar or selective schools, with the estimated coefficient actually being negative in each cohort, though statistically insignificant. Thus, earlier analyses showed that pupils from grammar/selective schools were less likely to play truant than pupils from comprehensive schools. However, once they have truanted and failed to reach the five or more GCSE benchmark, pupils from the former schools are no more likely to get back on track by participating in post-compulsory education than pupils from the latter schools.

Experience of career classes or interviews, and of work experience, are again positively and significantly related to good outcomes, in this case participating in post-compulsory full-time education, although it is not absolutely certain whether these results are the result of beneficial effects of the experiences themselves, or whether pupils more likely to continue their education are interested enough to self-select into such experiences.

There is some evidence for peer-group effects continuing in post-compulsory education; holding their own characteristics constant, the larger the percentage of pupils entitled to free school meals at former truants' former schools (Cohorts 8 and 9) or the larger the percentage of pupils statemented for special educational needs (Cohort 10), the less likely are former truants to continue in post-compulsory education. The size of class they experienced at school is again only weakly related to post-compulsory participation, although the coefficient for Cohort 10 is statistically significant, and suggests that former truants with experience of larger classes at school are less likely to participate in full-time learning after leaving school.

Finally, the additional variables included only in the Cohort 10 equation mostly yield statistically insignificant results, with the exception of the variable indicating frequent attendance at parents' evening, the positive coefficient on which shows that more parental interest is associated with a 9 percentage point higher probability of remaining in education.

The factors that affect the decision to continue in full-time education among very low-achieving (a failure to get five GCSEs at any grade) former truants are revealed in Table A4.6. The first thing to note is that the number of observations used to estimate the equations in this table is much smaller than before, as there are far fewer former truants who failed to get five GCSEs at any grade than who failed to get five GCSEs at Grade C or above. Some of the estimated coefficients on variables that only reflect a small proportion of this lower total number of observations (for example the ethnic minority indicators) will therefore be based on relatively few data points, and so may not be robust. Despite this, the characteristics of those who re-engage in further education from this group of very low-achieving former truants are quite similar to the characteristics of those who re-engage from the group of simply low-achieving former truants. Thus, from the very low-achieving group it is females and non-white (black and Asian) groups who are most likely to participate in full-time education, leaving white boys, as usual, the least likely to re-engage. The absence of a mother figure in the home is again important, this time in reducing participation. Family background seems less important when dealing with the very low-achieving former truants, however. The coefficients on the father's and mother's occupation variables are consistently statistically insignificant across all cohorts. This insignificance is not simply due to larger standard errors caused by smaller sample sizes in these equations, as the size of the father's occupation coefficients are consistently smaller than in previous tables, while the coefficients on the mother's occupation variable are actually negative in each cohort. In addition, none of the parental interest variables attract positive and statistically significant coefficients.

Table A4.7 repeats the same analysis as Table A4.5, but focusing only on serious truants who have failed to obtain five good GCSEs. The idea here is to see whether the factors identified above as helping re-engage former truants are still effective when the focus is switched to serious truants only. When making such comparisons between Table A4.7 and Table A4.5, it is important to look at the relative size of the coefficients, and not just at their statistical significance, since the considerably smaller sample size when attention is focused only on serious truants makes statistical significance harder to obtain.

Considering first the demographics, when attention is switched to former *serious* truants, there is less evidence that girls re-engage more than boys, with the exception of Cohort 9, where girls are still observed as being more likely to participate in post-compulsory education. The relative success of girls in re-engaging therefore seems to be due more to the behaviour of casual truants than more serious, regular offenders. With respect to ethnicity, however, most of the coefficients remain statistically significant, and of about the same order of magnitude as in Table A4.5, suggesting that the higher likelihood of ethnic minorities re-engaging, or the smaller likelihood of white pupils re-engaging, is true among the casual and the serious truant alike.

With respect to family background, the coefficients on the father's and mother's occupation variables are statistically significant in only one cohort each, although the absolute size of the coefficients is quite similar to those in Table A4.5. The influence of living in a privately owned home, or living with one's mother, do seem to be less than in Table A4.5, and so these characteristics, at least, are of less benefit in getting more serious truants to re-engage and participate in post-compulsory education. Parental interest also seems to have no beneficial effect on getting this group to re-engage. In general, putting results in this and the previous tables together, it might be argued that a good social background is less likely to help the more seriously disengaged back into education, where serious disengagement is measured by very low achievement (Table A4.6) or by serious truancy behaviour (Table A4.7).[30] It may be that the more seriously disengaged require more support than that provided by their family, if they are to be helped or persuaded into re-engagement.

30
Equations are not estimated for serious truants and very low-achievers together, since sample sizes would be getting very small in this case.

The remainder of the effects in Table A4.7, in particular the positive effects associated with careers services and work experience, and the negative effects associated with some peer groups, are very similar to those in Table A4.5. In general, therefore, most of the factors associated with truants deciding to get back into education remain relevant when the attention switches to more serious truants, with the possible exceptions of gender, and some of the social background indicators, the influence of which decline when we consider former serious truants.

Key points

Some former truants who failed to pass five or more good GCSEs nevertheless participate in post-compulsory education. They are more likely to do so if they:

- are female
- are from a non-white ethnic background
- have a higher socio-economic status
- live with (at least) their mother
- had careers interviews and work experience at school
- attended a school with fewer pupils with SEN or entitled to free school meals
- have supportive parents.

When looking at very low-achievers who fail to obtain five GCSEs at any level, or at pupils with serious truancy behaviour, most of these impacts are the same, with the exception that many of the social background indicators have a negligible impact on the re-engagement probabilities of these more disengaged groups.

What type of qualification is being studied for?

So far, what has been considered is whether individuals have been in full-time post-compulsory education, but not what is actually studied. However, this can be very important for future labour market prospects. There are three broad possibilities to be considered. First, individuals may be advancing their academic studies by taking A-levels. Second, they could be repeating their academic studies, presumably because of previous failures, by taking GCSEs. Finally, individuals could have left the academic stream and be studying for vocational qualifications. As the YCS contains detailed information about any courses being followed, so these three types of study can easily be identified. This is done in Table 4.5 and Figure 4.5, for each of the three cohorts separately and by truancy group.[31]

31
Note that the proportions in the three categories of study do not sum to the proportion in full-time education presented above for two reasons. First, the three types of study considered here are not mutually exclusive, so that individuals could be taking courses for vocational qualifications and GCSE resits, for example. Second, anyone studying for a qualification in one of these groups is included here, including those studying part-time, who would not have been included in the previous section, which looked at participation in full-time education only.

Table 4.5
Percentage attending different courses, by truancy category and cohort
Data source: Youth Cohort Study

	Low-achieving truants	Low-achieving serious truants	All others
Cohort 8			
A-levels	5.8	2.8	63.7
GCSEs	18.6	11.9	18.8
Vocational qualifications	53.7	42.2	33.2
Cohort 9			
A-levels	4.0	2.9	59.1
GCSEs	12.0	8.2	14.7
Vocational qualifications	50.6	37.8	34.3
Cohort 10			
A-levels	5.5	2.7	59.8
GCSEs	12.3	9.7	12.0
Vocational qualifications	52.5	41.6	36.1

These results show that among former truants who have failed to obtain five or more good GCSEs, few (only 4–6%) are studying for A-levels in the year following compulsory schooling. This is not surprising, given that the five or more GCSEs at Grades A*–C is widely used as an entry requirement for advanced level study. However, the academic stream as a whole does not seem popular with this group, since only 19% of them in Cohort 8, and only 12% in both Cohorts 9 and 10, are re-taking GCSE courses. Instead, study towards vocational qualifications is most popular among this group, being undertaken by just over half of the individuals in this group.

Looking at the group of low-achieving former serious truants, the differences are even more stark, with only around 3% of this group studying for A-levels, and around 10% studying for GCSEs. About 40% of this group are studying for vocational qualifications (less than the proportion among all truants, since fewer of the former serious truants are undertaking any learning at all).

Figure 4.5
Percentage attending different courses,
by truancy category and cohort
Data source: Youth Cohort Study
■ = Low-achieving truants
■ = Low-achieving serious truants
□ = All others

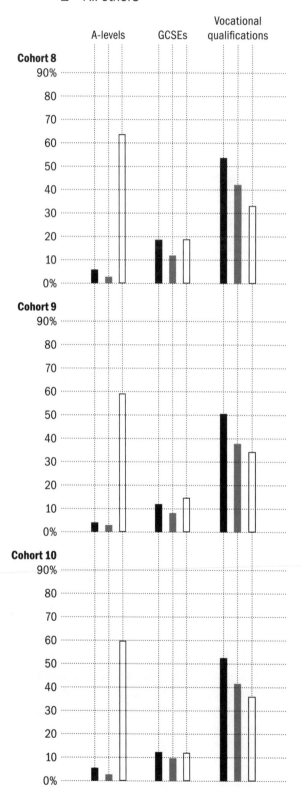

Finally, among the non-disengaged (who did not truant at school, or truanted but still obtained at least five good GCSEs), the most popular type of study is for A-levels, being followed by about 60% of this group. Between 12 and 19%, depending on cohort, are re-taking GCSEs. Finally, it is interesting to note that vocational studies are not the preserve of the previously low-achieving or disengaged, since around one-third of this most engaged group are also studying for vocational qualifications.

Very similar results are obtained when the very low-achieving (those failing to acquire five GCSEs at any grade) former truants are considered – rather than simply the low-achieving, who are much more inclined to study for vocational qualifications if in post-compulsory education. These results are therefore not set out in full.

Key points

■ Non-disengaged pupils at school are most likely to take A-levels if they remain in post-compulsory education.

■ Among those who truanted at school and failed to achieve five or more good GCSEs, very few do A-levels after compulsory education. While some do GCSE retakes, the most popular option, if learning is continued, is to study for vocational qualifications.

The factors associated with studying vocational qualifications

Since the focus of this chapter is on those who truanted in Year 11 and then failed to reach certain benchmarks in their GCSE exams, and since the previous subsection showed that members of this group, if they continue learning at all, are most likely to study for vocational qualifications, the remainder of this chapter will focus on this group of young people taking vocational courses.

This section aims to elicit through analyses the characteristics of those former truants who take vocational qualifications, compared to those who do not, to try to explain what it is that makes such people re-engage with education via a vocational route. The results of multivariate probit equations, with studying for a vocational qualification as the dependent variable, are presented in Tables A4.8 and A4.9, for low-achieving former truants and low-achieving former serious truants respectively.

32
Very low-achieving former truants are even more likely to be studying for vocational qualifications if participating in post-compulsory education, and thus the factors associated with vocational qualification study for this group are virtually the same as the factors associated with full-time education participation, as shown in Table A4.6, and so will not be discussed again here.

The characteristics associated with learning towards vocational qualifications are very similar to those associated with involvement in full-time education in general terms. Of course, this could have been predicted, given that the majority of former truants who continue their learning do so via vocational courses, so that, among the low-achieving former truants, those in full-time education and those studying for vocational qualifications, if not synonymous, overlap to a large extent. Thus if certain factors persuade a former truant to re-engage with learning (as discussed in the previous section), then they are more likely than not to go for a vocational option, which suggests that those same factors are associated with vocational learning.[32]

Thus in Table A4.8, among former truants who failed to obtain at least five good GCSEs, non-white ethnic groups are more likely than white pupils to be doing a vocational course. Additionally, living in a privately owned home, having a maternal figure in the home, attending careers interviews and attending work experience are all associated with higher probabilities of studying for vocational qualifications. However, the female, professional occupation father and professional occupation mother coefficients are all positive and statistically significant in only one of the three cohorts, and in general the size of these effects on vocational study seem to be smaller than those on full-time education in general. Thus, there is some evidence that although former disengaged girls and individuals from high socio-economic backgrounds are more likely to re-engage in post-compulsory education, they are not much more likely to be taking vocational qualifications, and so must be proportionally more likely to have re-engaged via academic qualifications.

Table A4.9 shows the characteristics associated with vocational study among low-achieving former serious truants. As was observed with respect to participation in full-time education in general, most of the factors associated with the re-engagement of former serious truants are similar to the factors associated with the re-engagement of all former truants. The clearest exception is the home ownership variable. Whereas former truants living in a privately owned home are more likely to undertake vocational qualifications, former serious truants living in a privately owned home are no more likely to undertake vocational qualifications than those living in rented accommodation. The tentative suggestion therefore again emerges that coming from a better-off family can help re-engage some former truants, but that the most serious truants are not really helped by having a good background.

Key points

Among former truants, characteristics associated with participation in vocational learning are similar to those associated with participation in full-time education in general. Therefore, those more likely to study for vocational qualifications among former truants are:

- females
- those from a non-white ethnic background
- those from a higher socio-economic status
  (though becoming less important than when explaining participation in full-time education in general)
- those who live with (at least) their mother
- those who had careers interviews and work experience at school
- those who attended a school with fewer pupils with SEN
- those with supportive parents.

What are the levels of achievement in post-compulsory education?

Finally, this chapter considers outcomes of the learning identified above. To do this, we have to look at subsequent sweeps of data collection in the YCS, and in particular use answers from surveys given to respondents two years after the initial involvement in the YCS, when the respondents are aged 18 or 19 (Sweep 2 of Cohort 8 and Sweep 3 of Cohorts 9 and 10).[33] Table 4.6 and Figure 4.6 show the highest academic qualifications obtained by the time of the later survey sweep, by cohort and truancy category.

The results predictably show that those who truanted at school and failed to acquire five or more good GCSEs are very unlikely to have acquired any A-levels or reached the five or more good GCSE benchmark two years later when they are aged 18 or 19. Among the non-disengaged (those who did not truant, or truanted but still achieved at least five good GCSEs), however, over half in each cohort go on to acquire at least two A-levels.

33
One issue that has been identified when using multiple sweeps in the YCS, but is difficult to control for, is attrition from the survey, such that not all individuals who initially responded to the YCS do so in later sweeps. To the extent that such dropping out of the survey is related to variables of interest, then this can affect any results obtained. For example, if individuals who are not successful in their post-compulsory education are less likely to respond to the YCS, then this could bias upwards any results on achievement, since successful students would be over-represented in the sample who remain in later sweeps of the YCS.

Table 4.6
Percentage obtaining highest academic qualification, by truancy category and cohort
Data source: Youth Cohort Study

	Low-achieving truants	Low-achieving serious truants	All others
Cohort 8			
2+ A-levels	1.75	1.65	50.33
1 A-level%	1.82	0.71	6.02
5+ GCSEs A*–C	3.98	1.18	25.51
1–4 GCSEs A*–C	54.54	44.10	11.92
5+ GCSEs D–G	25.70	29.01	4.63
1–4 GCSEs D–G	5.03	8.49	0.76
None reported	7.19	14.86	0.85
Cohort 9			
2+ A-levels	2.60	2.86	50.76
1 A-level	1.44	1.90	5.77
5+ GCSEs A*–C	7.94	6.19	26.95
1–4 GCSEs A*–C	63.78	60.00	12.00
5+ GCSEs D–G	18.47	20.95	3.60
1–4 GCSEs D–G	3.90	5.71	1.00
None reported	1.88	2.38	0.25
Cohort 10			
2+ A-levels	1.53	0.74	54.10
1 A-level	1.88	2.21	6.08
5+ GCSEs A*–C	2.12	0.37	22.65
1–4 GCSEs A*–C	58.30	48.90	11.98
No GCSEs A*–C	36.16	47.79	5.20

Figure 4.6
Percentage obtaining highest academic qualification,
by truancy category and cohort
Data source: Youth Cohort Study
■ = Low-achieving truants
■ = Low-achieving serious truants
□ = All others

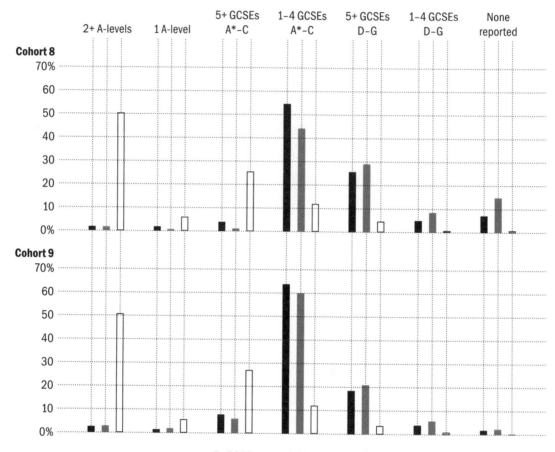

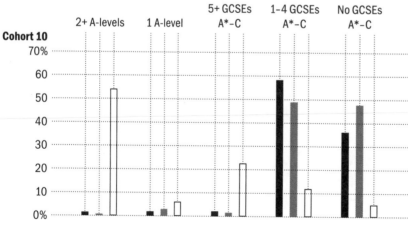

The use of the later sweeps of the YCS from this point until the end of this chapter makes it very difficult to examine the *very* low-achieving group. As was noted above, only a small proportion of the population falls into the category of former truant and very low-achiever, and given that the later sweeps of the YCS are affected by data attrition, leaving a smaller number of observations, then there are simply not sufficient observations to reliably investigate this group in the later sweeps of the YCS. The figures that emerge, however (not tabulated here due to imprecision) show that over 50% of this group of very low-achieving truants do not report any academic qualifications at the time of the follow-up survey.

Of more interest to this study are results in vocational learning. Because of the wide range of vocational qualifications available, the results, in Table 4.7 and Figure 4.7, are not given for individual qualifications, but for the National Qualifications Framework (NQF) level achieved.

Table 4.7
Percentage reaching highest NQF level via vocational qualifications, by truancy category and cohort
Data source: Youth Cohort Study

	Low-achieving truants	Low-achieving serious truants	All others
Cohort 8			
Level 4	7.94	8.09	6.85
Level 3	29.85	23.24	10.21
Level 2	10.08	5.22	10.44
Level 1	0.46	0.52	0.09
< Level 1	1.15	2.35	0.37
None	50.53	60.57	72.03
Cohort 9			
Level 4	0.00	0.00	0.10
Level 3	10.17	5.38	11.66
Level 2	35.05	33.33	12.90
Level 1	11.11	8.06	8.19
< Level 1	0.47	0.54	0.61
None	43.19	52.69	66.52
Cohort 10			
Level 4	0.00	0.00	0.00
Level 3	9.42	7.35	10.24
Level 2	26.15	22.06	11.58
Level 1	8.95	9.56	4.25
< Level 1	4.95	5.15	5.87
None	50.53	55.88	68.07

Figure 4.7
Percentage reaching highest NQF level via vocational qualifications,
by truancy category and cohort
■ = Low-achieving truants
■ = Low-achieving serious truants
□ = All others

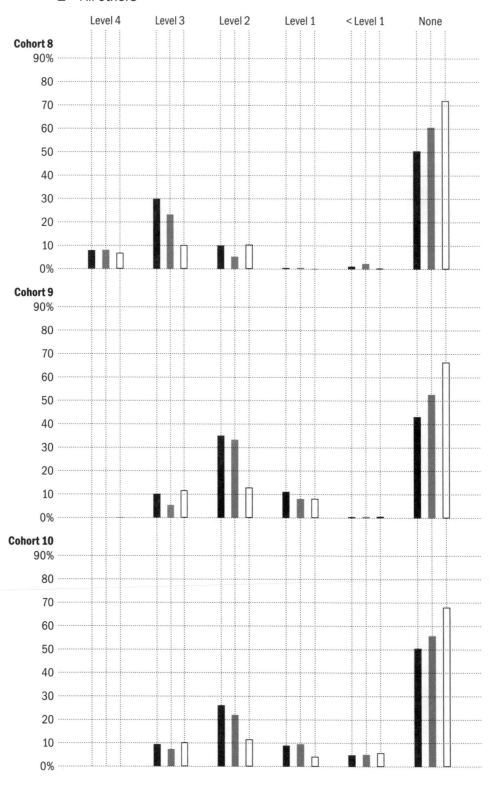

The results here show that the majority of young people do not acquire any vocational qualifications, this being particularly the case among those we have defined as non-disengaged, which is to be expected given their greater tendency for academic qualifications.

Focusing on those who have previously played truant, there seems to have been some definitional change in the survey between cohorts that requires further investigation, in that Cohort 8 reports significant numbers acquiring Level 4 and Level 3 vocational qualifications, while Cohorts 9 and 10 report no Level 4 qualifications and reduced numbers of Level 3 qualifications, but much higher numbers of Level 2 qualifications. The most consistent outcome to look at across cohorts therefore seems to be the proportion of individuals who achieve at least Level 2 via vocational qualifications.[34] The results reveal 36–48% of former truants who failed to achieve Level 2 via the academic route (ie five or more Grade A*–C GCSEs) reaching at least Level 2 via the vocational route. Therefore vocational qualifications represent a viable second chance to acquire a Level 2 qualification for significant numbers of individuals who (according to definitions used in this study) become disengaged while in school. Considering only the more serious, regular truants who failed to reach the five good GCSE benchmark, again we see 29–39%, according to cohort, re-engaging sufficiently to acquire at least a Level 2 vocational qualification.

There are again too few observations on very low-achieving former truants in the later sweeps of the YCS to accurately estimate the vocational qualification acquisitions of this group. However, it seems clear that the true level of acquisition will be very low, with the limited data available here suggesting that over 80% of very low-achieving former truants (and about 90% of very low-achieving former serious truants) acquire no vocational qualifications after compulsory schooling.

34
Another reason for focusing on the Level 2+ group is that Level 2 is widely considered to be the minimum requirement necessary to function in the modern labour market.

Key points

■ Former truants who failed to acquire at least five good GCSEs are very unlikely to obtain A-levels in the two years following completion of compulsory schooling.

■ Only small numbers of this group acquire GCSEs through resits during this period.

■ Significant numbers, up to about half of all former low-achieving truants, reach Level 2 via vocational qualifications over the same time period.

■ Of the very low-achieving former truants, however, very few (about 15%) acquire any vocational qualifications during this period.

Who succeeds in vocational education?

The previous section revealed that significant numbers of former truants manage to acquire meaningful vocational qualifications in the years following compulsory education. The final task of this chapter is to investigate the characteristics of former truants who successfully reach at least Level 2 via vocational qualifications, to see if some of the factors associated with their success can be identified. This is done in Tables A4.10 and A4.11, for all truants and only serious truants respectively.[35] In each case the estimating equation is again a probit, with the dependent variable being a dichotomous variable indicating the achievement of Level 2 or otherwise.[36]

The results in Tables A4.10 and A4.11 reveal very few statistically significant findings, which may be due to the sample sizes now getting quite small. The significant findings that emerge, considering all former low-achieving truants in Table A4.10 first, suggest, once again, that girls are more successful than boys in obtaining qualifications, being 5–11 percentage points more likely to reach Level 2 via vocational qualifications. Most of the ethnicity coefficients are positive, suggesting higher achievement among all other groups relative to white pupils, although the estimates are very poorly determined, and none achieve statistical significance.

Turning to family background, the influence of a good family background has become gradually weaker over consecutive analyses presented in this chapter, starting at GCSE success, and any full-time post-compulsory education participation, and finishing with vocational learning and achievement of vocational qualifications. Thus the benefit of a good background is less important for the achievement of vocational qualifications than it appeared to be for GCSE attainment, for instance. Nevertheless, most of the coefficients on variables indicating parents in senior occupations and residence in a privately owned home remain positive in the vocational qualification achievement equations, and occasionally are statistically significant (for example, living in a private residence for Cohort 10). Similarly, the importance of still living with one's parents (now measured at the time of the subsequent data collection and not at the first sweep as used above) is lower for vocational qualification acquisition than for outcomes reported earlier in this chapter, although it still remains the case that individuals living on their own, without either parent, are the least likely to reach Level 2 via vocational qualifications, even if most of the coefficients are statistically insignificant. Finally, of the variables that can be considered in Cohort 10 only, the results suggest that individuals who received a statement of SEN while at school are 16 percentage points less likely to reach Level 2 via vocational qualifications, while the influence of supportive parents can still be observed, with individuals whose parents attended most of their parents' evenings at school being 11 percentage points more likely to reach Level 2 via vocational qualifications.

In Table A4.11, for former serious truants only, there are virtually no statistically significant coefficients, although to the extent that there is any pattern in the estimated coefficients, they are largely consistent with those obtained for all former truants in Table A4.10.

35
Sample sizes were definitely too small to do any meaningful analysis of very low-achieving former truants in this context.

36
One question to be decided was whether to limit the sample to all those who had said they were studying for vocational qualifications in Sweep 1 of the survey, since those studying only for academic qualifications necessarily will fail to acquire a Level 2 vocational qualification. It was decided not to do this, and keep the samples as all former low-achieving truants and low-achieving serious truants respectively, since by limiting the sample only to learners at the time of the Sweep 1 survey, this would have excluded all those who had started learning, and may have been successful, after the first survey was conducted. Furthermore, as shown in Table 4.4 and Figure 4.4, very few former low-achieving truants are studying for academic qualifications in any case.

Key points

Very few factors are significantly associated with former low-achieving truants nevertheless achieving Level 2 via vocational qualifications. The ones that are so associated suggest a higher likelihood of such achievement for:

■ females

■ non-white ethnic groups (tentatively, given a lack of statistical significance)

■ those from a higher socio-economic background (though this factor appears much less important than it was in explaining, for example, GCSE attainment earlier)

■ those still living with at least one parent

■ those without SEN

■ those with supportive parents.

Conclusion

This chapter set out to analyse some of the effects of disengagement in school on future outcomes, and the characteristics associated with differences in such outcomes. The definition of disengagement used depended on data available in large-scale data sets. In the end, a variable indicating those who had played truant during Year 11 at school was chosen. The first results of this chapter showed that such truants achieved lower GCSE results on average, with the results being worse depending on the extent (frequency or regularity) of truancy behaviour. Nevertheless, a significant proportion of truants still achieved five or more good GCSEs, suggesting that they were unlikely to have actually disengaged. From this point on, the analyses undertaken therefore used as an indicator of disengagement those who played truant and failed to acquire five or more good GCSEs (or five at any grade).

The results suggest that former disengaged pupils, as defined here, are less likely to continue in post-compulsory education. This is particularly the case for white boys, with other groups being more likely to re-engage by restarting learning. Social background is also important here, with those from a higher socio-economic background being more likely to re-engage. Having supportive parents, and living with parents, are also both related to the probability of re-engaging. However, a good social background is less likely to influence re-engagement among more seriously disengaged young people, who either consistently (seriously) truanted or who failed to acquire five GCSEs even at Grade G. The answer to re-engaging these groups probably lies outside the family.

When the previously disengaged do re-engage, it is most likely to be via vocational learning. Although a significant minority take GCSE resits, very few enter for A-levels. For a significant number (up to half), this re-engagement in education via vocational learning can have good outcomes, in particular reaching Level 2 in the National Qualifications Framework. It seems that girls, and possibly non-white pupils and those from higher socio-economic backgrounds, are more likely to be successful in this regard. The next chapter focuses on the impact such vocational qualification acquisition has on labour market outcomes for this group.

Regression appendix

Table A4.1
Factors associated with obtaining five or more good GCSEs
Data source: Youth Cohort Study
Robust standard errors are shown in parentheses
* = Coefficient significant at 5% ** = Coefficient significant at 1%

Variable	Cohort 8		Cohort 9		Cohort 10		Cohort 10	
Ever played truant	−0.190	(0.010)**	−0.203	(0.011)**	−0.192	(0.011)**	−0.183	(0.011)**
Female	0.098	(0.010)**	0.096	(0.010)**	0.096	(0.010)**	0.083	(0.010)**
Black	−0.028	(0.046)	−0.021	(0.041)	0.016	(0.036)	0.020	(0.037)
Asian	0.107	(0.021)**	0.135	(0.020)**	0.105	(0.019)**	0.117	(0.019)**
Other ethnic group	0.085	(0.038)*	0.111	(0.039)**	−0.045	(0.053)	−0.060	(0.054)
Senior occupation father	0.169	(0.011)**	0.152	(0.011)**	0.133	(0.011)**	0.127	(0.011)**
Father's occupation missing	−0.064	(0.016)**	−0.028	(0.016)	−0.031	(0.015)*	−0.034	(0.016)*
Senior occupation mother	0.112	(0.012)**	0.132	(0.012)**	0.099	(0.011)**	0.101	(0.012)**
Mother's occupation missing	−0.029	(0.013)*	−0.062	(0.014)**	−0.028	(0.014)*	−0.024	(0.015)
Live in privately owned home	0.184	(0.014)**	0.170	(0.015)**	0.203	(0.014)**	0.177	(0.015)**
Not living with father	−0.001	(0.016)	−0.008	(0.015)	0.006	(0.015)	0.009	(0.015)
Not living with mother	−0.092	(0.022)**	−0.046	(0.023)**	−0.062	(0.023)**	−0.040	(0.024)
Number of siblings	−0.022	(0.004)**	−0.014	(0.004)**	−0.022	(0.005)**	−0.019	(0.005)**
Independent school	0.201	(0.035)**	0.099	(0.111)**				
Secondary modern school	−0.130	(0.026)**	−0.127	(0.028)**	−0.097	(0.031)**	−0.077	(0.032)*
Grammar/selective school	0.353	(0.020)**	0.373	(0.015)**	0.310	(0.018)**	0.311	(0.016)**
Had careers classes	0.151	(0.018)**	0.051	(0.016)**	0.056	(0.015)**	0.049	(0.015)**
Had own careers interview	−0.031	(0.016)*	−0.086	(0.021)**	0.083	(0.019)**	0.072	(0.020)**
Had work experience in Year 11	0.069	(0.029)*	0.038	(0.028)	0.109	(0.024)**	0.094	(0.025)**
Average class size	−0.004	(0.003)	0.002	(0.003)	0.005	(0.003)*	0.005	(0.003)
% eligible for free school meals	−0.595	(0.058)**	−0.632	(0.053)**	−0.527	(0.061)**	−0.550	(0.063)**
% SEN with statement	−0.969	(0.347)**	−0.018	(0.023)	−1.023	(0.337)**	−0.718	(0.369)
% SEN without statement	−0.102	(0.069)	−0.020	(0.047)	−0.248	(0.075)**	−0.234	(0.077)**
Identified as having SEN							−0.265	(0.026)**
Received a statement of SEN							−0.157	(0.032)**
Previously been in residential or foster care							−0.083	(0.048)
Parents always/frequently attended parents' evenings							0.155	(0.018)**
Parents read to children every night or often							0.057	(0.011)**
Frequent parental help with examination options, etc							−0.026	(0.011)*
Observations	12,518		11,203		10,848		10,505	

Table A4.2
Factors associated with obtaining five or more GCSEs at any grade
Data source: Youth Cohort Study
Robust standard errors are shown in parentheses
* = Coefficient significant at 5%   ** = Coefficient significant at 1%

Variable	Cohort 8		Cohort 9		Cohort 10		Cohort 10	
Ever played truant	−0.044	(0.004)**	−0.051	(0.005)**	−0.036	(0.004)**	−0.028	(0.004)**
Female	0.016	(0.004)**	0.012	(0.004)**	0.018	(0.004)**	0.013	(0.003)**
Black	0.011	(0.010)	0.030	(0.007)**	−0.003	(0.012)	−0.006	(0.012)
Asian	0.023	(0.005)**	0.035	(0.004)**	0.024	(0.004)**	0.020	(0.004)**
Other ethnic group	0.030	(0.007)**	0.038	(0.006)**	−0.004	(0.019)	−0.007	(0.018)
Senior occupation father	0.023	(0.004)**	0.026	(0.005)**	0.022	(0.004)**	0.020	(0.004)**
Father's occupation missing	−0.027	(0.006)**	−0.019	(0.006)**	−0.013	(0.005)*	−0.010	(0.005)*
Senior occupation mother	0.017	(0.004)**	0.024	(0.005)**	0.015	(0.004)**	0.014	(0.004)**
Mother's occupation missing	−0.006	(0.004)	−0.017	(0.006)**	−0.009	(0.005)	−0.008	(0.004)
Live in privately owned home	0.040	(0.006)**	0.046	(0.007)**	0.030	(0.006)**	0.022	(0.005)**
Not living with father	−0.002	(0.005)	−0.009	(0.006)	−0.005	(0.005)	−0.006	(0.005)
Not living with mother	−0.042	(0.009)**	−0.022	(0.009)*	−0.019	(0.008)*	−0.012	(0.007)
Number of siblings	−0.003	(0.001)**	−0.004	(0.002)*	−0.005	(0.002)**	−0.004	(0.001)**
Independent school			0.008	(0.025)				
Secondary modern school	−0.024	(0.011)*	−0.002	(0.011)	−0.005	(0.010)	−0.003	(0.008)
Grammar/selective school	0.029	(0.007)**	0.038	(0.008)**	0.020	(0.008)**	0.015	(0.008)*
Had careers classes	0.063	(0.010)**	0.039	(0.008)**	0.026	(0.006)**	0.022	(0.006)**
Had own careers interview	0.060	(0.008)**	0.082	(0.012)**	0.046	(0.008)**	0.041	(0.008)**
Had work experience in Year 11	0.068	(0.013)**	0.076	(0.014)**	0.047	(0.010)**	0.039	(0.009)**
Average class size	−0.000	(0.001)	0.001	(0.001)	−0.000	(0.001)	−0.001	(0.001)
% eligible for free school meals	−0.103	(0.015)**	−0.130	(0.016)**	−0.090	(0.019)**	−0.082	(0.018)**
% SEN with statement	−0.108	(0.092)	−0.003	(0.008)	−0.264	(0.105)*	−0.186	(0.105)
% SEN without statement	−0.006	(0.020)	0.014	(0.017)	−0.016	(0.022)	−0.013	(0.020)
Identified as having SEN							−0.033	(0.012)**
Received a statement of SEN							−0.041	(0.014)**
Previously been in residential or foster care							−0.013	(0.014)
Parents always/frequently attended parents' evenings							0.033	(0.007)**
Parents read to children every night or often							0.002	(0.004)
Frequent parental help with examination options, etc							−0.007	(0.003)*
Observations	12,586		11,203		10,848		10,505	

Table A4.3
Factors associated with obtaining five or more good GCSEs
Data source: Youth Cohort Study
Robust standard errors are shown in parentheses
* = Coefficient significant at 5%　** = Coefficient significant at 1%

Variable	Cohort 8		Cohort 9		Cohort 10		Cohort 10	
Played serious truant	-0.286	(0.016)**	-0.337	(0.016)**	-0.362	(0.019)**	-0.340	(0.021)**
Female	0.093	(0.010)**	0.094	(0.010)**	0.090	(0.010)**	0.076	(0.010)**
Black	-0.033	(0.046)	0.019	(0.041)	0.014	(0.037)	0.018	(0.039)
Asian	0.101	(0.021)**	0.142	(0.020)**	0.106	(0.019)**	0.121	(0.020)**
Other ethnic group	0.081	(0.038)*	0.121	(0.040)**	-0.050	(0.052)	-0.064	(0.054)
Senior occupation father	0.171	(0.011)**	0.155	(0.011)**	0.137	(0.011)**	0.130	(0.011)**
Father's occupation missing	-0.063	(0.016)**	-0.028	(0.016)	-0.033	(0.015)*	-0.037	(0.016)*
Senior occupation mother	0.107	(0.012)**	0.133	(0.012)**	0.101	(0.011)**	0.102	(0.012)**
Mother's occupation missing	-0.023	(0.013)	-0.059	(0.014)**	-0.023	(0.014)	-0.019	(0.015)
Live in privately owned home	0.181	(0.014)**	0.166	(0.015)**	0.200	(0.015)**	0.173	(0.015)**
Not living with father	-0.010	(0.016)	-0.013	(0.015)	0.005	(0.015)	0.008	(0.015)
Not living with mother	-0.092	(0.022)**	-0.038	(0.023)	-0.068	(0.023)**	-0.044	(0.024)
Number of siblings	-0.023	(0.004)**	-0.016	(0.004)**	-0.023	(0.005)**	-0.019	(0.005)**
Independent school	0.207	(0.045)**	0.112	(0.107)				
Secondary modern school	-0.122	(0.025)**	-0.123	(0.027)**	-0.094	(0.031)**	-0.072	(0.033)*
Grammar/selective school	0.361	(0.020)**	0.375	(0.016)**	0.314	(0.018)**	0.315	(0.016)**
Had careers classes	0.146	(0.019)**	0.045	(0.016)**	0.059	(0.015)**	0.053	(0.016)**
Had own careers interview	-0.034	(0.016)*	0.073	(0.021)**	0.071	(0.019)**	0.059	(0.020)**
Had work experience in Year 11	0.065	(0.029)*	0.029	(0.029)	0.099	(0.024)**	0.084	(0.025)**
Average class size	-0.003	(0.003)	0.002	(0.003)	0.006	(0.003)*	0.006	(0.003)*
% eligible for free school meals	-0.604	(0.057)**	-0.641	(0.054)**	-0.516	(0.062)**	-0.537	(0.065)**
% SEN with statement	-0.977	(0.343)**	-0.015	(0.023)	-1.042	(0.338)**	-0.725	(0.372)
% SEN without statement	-0.094	(0.067)	0.029	(0.046)	-0.231	(0.075)**	-0.220	(0.077)**
Identified as having SEN							-0.262	(0.026)**
Received a statement of SEN							-0.151	(0.032)**
Previously been in residential or foster care							-0.074	(0.049)
Parents always/frequently attended parents' evenings							0.157	(0.019)**
Parents read to children every night or often							0.063	(0.011)**
Frequent parental help with examination options, etc							-0.020	(0.011)
Observations	12,518		11,203		10,848		10,505	

Table A4.4
Factors associated with obtaining five or more GCSEs at any grade
Data source: Youth Cohort Study
Robust standard errors are shown in parentheses
* = Coefficient significant at 5%   ** = Coefficient significant at 1%

Variable	Cohort 8		Cohort 9		Cohort 10		Cohort 10	
Played serious truant	-0.119	(0.010)**	-0.129	(0.012)**	-0.097	(0.011)**	-0.082	(0.011)**
Female	0.016	(0.004)**	0.013	(0.004)**	0.017	(0.004)**	0.013	(0.003)**
Black	0.011	(0.010)	0.030	(0.007)**	-0.003	(0.012)	-0.007	(0.013)
Asian	0.022	(0.005)**	0.036	(0.004)**	0.024	(0.004)**	0.020	(0.004)**
Other ethnic group	0.029	(0.007)**	0.038	(0.006)**	-0.009	(0.020)	-0.011	(0.019)
Senior occupation father	0.022	(0.004)**	0.025	(0.005)**	0.022	(0.004)**	0.020	(0.004)**
Father's occupation missing	-0.026	(0.006)**	-0.018	(0.006)**	-0.014	(0.006)*	-0.012	(0.005)*
Senior occupation mother	0.016	(0.004)**	0.025	(0.005)**	0.015	(0.004)**	0.014	(0.004)**
Mother's occupation missing	-0.006	(0.004)	-0.017	(0.005)**	-0.008	(0.005)	-0.007	(0.004)
Live in privately owned home	0.035	(0.005)**	0.043	(0.007)**	0.028	(0.005)**	0.021	(0.005)**
Not living with father	-0.003	(0.005)	-0.009	(0.006)	-0.004	(0.005)	-0.004	(0.005)
Not living with mother	-0.036	(0.009)**	-0.015	(0.008)	-0.016	(0.008)*	-0.010	(0.007)
Number of siblings	-0.003	(0.001)**	-0.004	(0.002)**	-0.005	(0.002)**	-0.004	(0.001)**
Independent school			0.007	(0.023)				
Secondary modern school	-0.022	(0.011)*	-0.003	(0.012)	-0.003	(0.009)	-0.001	(0.008)
Grammar/selective school	0.030	(0.006)**	0.037	(0.008)**	0.021	(0.007)**	0.015	(0.007)*
Had careers classes	0.057	(0.009)**	0.036	(0.007)**	0.026	(0.006)**	0.022	(0.006)**
Had own careers interview	0.056	(0.008)**	0.074	(0.011)**	0.038	(0.008)**	0.033	(0.007)**
Had work experience in Year 11	0.062	(0.013)**	0.067	(0.014)**	0.042	(0.010)**	0.035	(0.009)**
Average class size	0.000	(0.001)	0.001	(0.001)	0.000	(0.001)	-0.000	(0.001)
% eligible for free school meals	-0.104	(0.015)**	-0.128	(0.016)**	-0.088	(0.019)**	-0.080	(0.018)**
% SEN with statement	-0.095	(0.094)	-0.003	(0.008)	-0.269	(0.099)**	-0.192	(0.099)
% SEN without statement	-0.004	(0.020)	0.016	(0.017)	-0.013	(0.022)	-0.010	(0.020)
Identified as having SEN							-0.033	(0.011)**
Received a statement of SEN							-0.039	(0.014)**
Previously been in residential or foster care							-0.009	(0.013)
Parents always/frequently attended parents' evenings							0.030	(0.006)**
Parents read to children every night or often							0.003	(0.004)
Frequent parental help with examination options, etc							-0.006	(0.003)
Observations	12,586		11,203		10,848		10,505	

Table A4.5
Determinants of being in full-time education among low-achieving former truants
Data source: Youth Cohort Study
Robust standard errors are shown in parentheses
* = Coefficient significant at 5%   ** = Coefficient significant at 1%

Variable	Cohort 8		Cohort 9		Cohort 10		Cohort 10	
Female	0.085	(0.021)**	0.087	(0.022)**	0.070	(0.024)**	0.073	(0.025)**
Black	0.324	(0.053)**	0.276	(0.069)**	0.229	(0.076)**	0.209	(0.079)**
Asian	0.329	(0.037)**	0.391	(0.043)**	0.299	(0.050)**	0.294	(0.051)**
Other ethnic group	0.293	(0.068)**	0.373	(0.081)**	0.221	(0.096)*	0.199	(0.098)*
Senior occupation father	0.114	(0.029)**	0.136	(0.030)**	0.012	(0.033)	0.011	(0.034)
Father's occupation missing	0.034	(0.029)	0.040	(0.029)	0.040	(0.033)	0.034	(0.033)
Senior occupation mother	0.076	(0.031)*	0.091	(0.034)**	0.046	(0.035)	0.041	(0.035)
Mother's occupation missing	−0.003	(0.027)	0.064	(0.027)*	−0.010	(0.031)	−0.010	(0.031)
Live in privately owned home	0.079	(0.024)**	0.079	(0.025)**	0.110	(0.027)**	0.103	(0.028)**
Not living with father	0.017	(0.030)	0.018	(0.029)	−0.025	(0.033)	−0.014	(0.034)
Not living with mother	−0.154	(0.036)**	−0.167	(0.033)**	−0.124	(0.040)**	−0.127	(0.041)**
Number of siblings	0.006	(0.007)	−0.003	(0.008)	−0.006	(0.011)	−0.005	(0.011)
Independent school			0.194	(0.157)				
Secondary modern school	−0.100	(0.047)*	−0.091	(0.051)	0.003	(0.055)	−0.002	(0.059)
Grammar/selective school	−0.014	(0.142)	−0.017	(0.156)	−0.272	(0.166)	−0.154	(0.203)
Had careers classes	0.102	(0.033)**	0.098	(0.031)**	0.027	(0.030)	0.025	(0.031)
Had own careers interview	0.115	(0.032)**	0.182	(0.033)**	0.086	(0.034)*	0.082	(0.035)*
Had work experience in Year 11	0.109	(0.041)**	0.068	(0.043)	0.092	(0.038)*	0.092	(0.039)*
Average class size	−0.005	(0.005)	−0.003	(0.006)	−0.015	(0.006)**	−0.015	(0.006)*
% eligible for free school meals	−0.256	(0.101)*	−0.198	(0.093)*	−0.122	(0.124)	−0.119	(0.127)
% SEN with statement	−0.454	(0.635)	0.013	(0.045)	−1.606	(0.635)*	−1.587	(0.662)*
% SEN without statement	−0.028	(0.114)	−0.021	(0.098)	−0.040	(0.155)	−0.052	(0.159)
Identified as having SEN							0.007	(0.049)
Received a statement of SEN							0.012	(0.053)
Previously been in residential or foster care							0.028	(0.075)
Parents always/frequently attended parents' evenings							0.090	(0.029)**
Parents read to children every night or often							−0.030	(0.028)
Frequent parental help with examination options, etc							−0.004	(0.027)
Observations	2,586		2,302		1,864		1,795	

Table A4.6
Determinants of being in full-time education among very low-achieving former truants
Data source: Youth Cohort Study
Robust standard errors are shown in parentheses
* = Coefficient significant at 5%   ** = Coefficient significant at 1%

Variable	Cohort 8		Cohort 9		Cohort 10		Cohort 10	
Female	0.076	(0.036)*	0.071	(0.035)*	0.088	(0.043)*	0.070	(0.046)
Black	0.365	(0.169)*	0.015	(0.171)	0.139	(0.137)	0.204	(0.152)
Asian	0.382	(0.119)**	0.330	(0.130)*	0.323	(0.141)*	0.319	(0.144)*
Other ethnic group	0.141	(0.184)	0.227	(0.248)	0.461	(0.266)	0.430	(0.265)
Senior occupation father	0.031	(0.069)	0.053	(0.066)	0.078	(0.078)	0.066	(0.081)
Father's occupation missing	0.008	(0.047)	-0.018	(0.042)	0.048	(0.057)	0.028	(0.058)
Senior occupation mother	-0.007	(0.068)	-0.017	(0.062)	-0.017	(0.062)	-0.032	(0.062)
Mother's occupation missing	-0.044	(0.041)	0.075	(0.042)	0.062	(0.055)	0.042	(0.056)
Live in privately owned home	-0.004	(0.039)	0.045	(0.037)	0.099	(0.047)*	0.087	(0.048)
Not living with father	0.007	(0.043)	0.054	(0.044)	0.022	(0.058)	0.037	(0.061)
Not living with mother	-0.125	(0.038)**	-0.052	(0.046)	-0.124	(0.052)*	-0.137	(0.050)**
Number of siblings	-0.011	(0.010)	0.014	(0.011)	-0.010	(0.018)	-0.015	(0.019)
Independent school			0.127	(0.215)				
Secondary modern school	0.069	(0.084)	-0.098	(0.058)	0.079	(0.116)	0.093	(0.117)
Grammar/selective school	0.113	(0.253)	0.180	(0.263)				
Had careers classes	0.033	(0.046)	0.070	(0.039)	0.053	(0.048)	0.062	(0.049)
Had own careers interview	0.103	(0.036)**	0.051	(0.040)	0.062	(0.047)	0.087	(0.047)
Had work experience in Year 11	-0.016	(0.049)	0.002	(0.050)	0.032	(0.054)	0.052	(0.054)
Average class size	0.007	(0.009)	-0.004	(0.009)	-0.001	(0.010)	-0.001	(0.010)
% eligible for free school meals	-0.099	(0.152)	-0.187	(0.133)	0.046	(0.218)	0.065	(0.222)
% SEN with statement	-2.426	(1.121)*	-0.019	(0.061)	-1.069	(1.297)	-0.862	(1.336)
% SEN without statement	0.158	(0.156)	-0.128	(0.155)	0.093	(0.236)	0.018	(0.244)
Identified as having SEN							0.088	(0.092)
Received a statement of SEN							-0.053	(0.074)
Previously been in residential or foster care							0.192	(0.147)
Parents always/frequently attended parents' evenings							-0.013	(0.049)
Parents read to children every night or often							-0.003	(0.053)
Frequent parental help with examination options, etc							-0.033	(0.051)
Observations	526		530		374		349	

Table A4.7
Determinants of being in full-time education
among low-achieving former serious truants
Data source: Youth Cohort Study
Robust standard errors are shown in parentheses
* = Coefficient significant at 5%　** = Coefficient significant at 1%

Variable	Cohort 8		Cohort 9		Cohort 10		Cohort 10	
Female	0.032	(0.035)	0.074	(0.032)*	0.020	(0.040)	0.034	(0.041)
Black	0.469	(0.093)**	0.205	(0.132)	0.210	(0.116)	0.183	(0.129)
Asian	0.389	(0.078)**	0.343	(0.097)**	0.285	(0.094)**	0.259	(0.097)**
Other ethnic group	0.353	(0.141)*	0.412	(0.161)*	0.118	(0.181)	0.108	(0.187)
Senior occupation father	0.081	(0.057)	0.162	(0.052)**	0.022	(0.053)	0.007	(0.055)
Father's occupation missing	0.025	(0.047)	0.023	(0.044)	0.112	(0.053)*	0.086	(0.055)
Senior occupation mother	0.114	(0.059)	0.111	(0.056)*	0.015	(0.054)	0.012	(0.056)
Mother's occupation missing	−0.003	(0.043)	0.077	(0.041)	0.010	(0.048)	0.005	(0.049)
Live in privately owned home	0.044	(0.038)	0.045	(0.037)	0.079	(0.042)	0.090	(0.043)*
Not living with father	0.047	(0.051)	0.024	(0.041)	−0.085	(0.046)	−0.063	(0.048)
Not living with mother	−0.107	(0.051)*	−0.107	(0.045)*	−0.047	(0.059)	−0.072	(0.059)
Number of siblings	0.006	(0.011)	0.015	(0.012)	0.003	(0.016)	−0.000	(0.016)
Independent school			0.234	(0.327)				
Secondary modern school	−0.118	(0.080)	−0.042	(0.077)	−0.053	(0.101)	−0.084	(0.097)
Grammar/selective school	−0.156	(0.128)						
Had careers classes	0.123	(0.049)*	0.032	(0.043)	0.076	(0.044)	0.077	(0.044)
Had own careers interview	0.122	(0.043)**	0.137	(0.039)**	0.122	(0.043)**	0.119	(0.043)**
Had work experience in Year 11	−0.037	(0.060)	0.009	(0.054)	0.079	(0.051)	0.080	(0.053)
Average class size	0.006	(0.008)	−0.001	(0.008)	0.008	(0.009)	0.004	(0.009)
% eligible for free school meals	−0.510	(0.167)**	−0.104	(0.143)	−0.208	(0.200)	−0.170	(0.207)
% SEN with statement	−1.685	(1.265)	−0.018	(0.077)	−2.802	(1.095)*	−2.862	(1.126)*
% SEN without statement	0.218	(0.189)	0.213	(0.140)	0.368	(0.251)	0.381	(0.257)
Identified as having SEN							0.013	(0.071)
Received a statement of SEN							−0.015	(0.075)
Previously been in residential or foster care							0.000	(0.101)
Parents always/frequently attended parents' evenings							0.050	(0.043)
Parents read to children every night or often							−0.098	(0.043)*
Frequent parental help with examination options, etc							0.006	(0.043)
Observations	855		824		667		640	

Table A4.8
Determinants of studying for vocational qualifications among low-achieving former truants
Data source: Youth Cohort Study
Robust standard errors are shown in parentheses
* = Coefficient significant at 5%   ** = Coefficient significant at 1%

Variable	Cohort 8		Cohort 9		Cohort 10		Cohort 10	
Female	0.025	(0.020)	0.079	(0.022)**	0.030	(0.025)	0.031	(0.025)
Black	0.185	(0.063)**	0.282	(0.065)**	0.111	(0.084)	0.104	(0.087)
Asian	0.075	(0.046)	0.141	(0.049)**	0.113	(0.056)*	0.120	(0.057)*
Other ethnic group	0.095	(0.082)	0.148	(0.093)	0.165	(0.097)	0.150	(0.098)
Senior occupation father	0.004	(0.029)	0.078	(0.031)*	0.010	(0.033)	0.015	(0.034)
Father's occupation missing	−0.007	(0.028)	0.039	(0.031)	0.005	(0.034)	0.011	(0.035)
Senior occupation mother	0.055	(0.031)	−0.017	(0.036)	0.090	(0.033)**	0.073	(0.034)*
Mother's occupation missing	−0.005	(0.026)	0.015	(0.027)	−0.039	(0.032)	−0.040	(0.033)
Live in privately owned home	0.097	(0.023)**	0.065	(0.026)*	0.061	(0.028)*	0.055	(0.029)
Not living with father	−0.007	(0.028)	−0.054	(0.029)	−0.041	(0.033)	−0.034	(0.034)
Not living with mother	−0.152	(0.036)**	−0.163	(0.037)**	−0.087	(0.041)*	−0.089	(0.043)*
Number of siblings	0.007	(0.007)	0.001	(0.007)	0.004	(0.011)	0.002	(0.011)
Independent school			−0.037	(0.154)				
Secondary modern school	0.068	(0.048)	−0.013	(0.055)	−0.031	(0.064)	−0.031	(0.066)
Grammar/selective school	−0.120	(0.141)	−0.195	(0.140)	−0.236	(0.264)	−0.269	(0.249)
Had careers classes	0.121	(0.034)**	0.069	(0.033)*	−0.014	(0.031)	−0.023	(0.031)
Had own careers interview	0.123	(0.031)**	0.197	(0.037)**	0.128	(0.037)**	0.125	(0.038)**
Had work experience in Year 11	0.102	(0.039)**	0.039	(0.044)	0.098	(0.039)*	0.103	(0.041)*
Average class size	0.003	(0.005)	−0.009	(0.005)	−0.001	(0.006)	−0.001	(0.006)
% eligible for free school meals	−0.125	(0.100)	−0.166	(0.095)	0.002	(0.126)	−0.011	(0.131)
% SEN with statement	−0.251	(0.621)	0.000	(0.043)	−1.415	(0.661)*	−1.205	(0.732)
% SEN without statement	−0.196	(0.121)	−0.071	(0.094)	−0.126	(0.154)	−0.159	(0.159)
Identified as having SEN							0.008	(0.050)
Received a statement of SEN							−0.003	(0.056)
Previously been in residential or foster care							0.052	(0.074)
Parents always/frequently attended parents' evenings							0.052	(0.029)
Parents read to children every night or often							−0.061	(0.028)*
Frequent parental help with examination options, etc							0.089	(0.027)**
Observations	2,575		2,158		1,773		1,712	

Table A4.9
**Determinants of studying for vocational qualifications
among low-achieving former serious truants**
Data source: Youth Cohort Study
Robust standard errors are shown in parentheses
* = Coefficient significant at 5%   ** = Coefficient significant at 1%

Variable	Cohort 8		Cohort 9		Cohort 10		Cohort 10	
Female	-0.028	(0.036)	0.085	(0.036)*	0.018	(0.042)	0.025	(0.044)
Black	0.279	(0.107)**	0.213	(0.136)	0.052	(0.130)	0.013	(0.138)
Asian	0.102	(0.083)	0.250	(0.091)**	0.045	(0.099)	0.059	(0.102)
Other ethnic group	0.072	(0.153)	0.140	(0.161)	0.021	(0.191)	-0.014	(0.189)
Senior occupation father	-0.053	(0.056)	0.184	(0.057)**	0.065	(0.057)	0.065	(0.059)
Father's occupation missing	-0.067	(0.047)	-0.011	(0.048)	0.075	(0.057)	0.073	(0.060)
Senior occupation mother	0.134	(0.058)*	-0.055	(0.058)	0.096	(0.060)	0.079	(0.060)
Mother's occupation missing	-0.002	(0.045)	0.022	(0.043)	-0.040	(0.051)	-0.061	(0.053)
Live in privately owned home	0.039	(0.040)	0.038	(0.040)	0.060	(0.046)	0.064	(0.047)
Not living with father	0.084	(0.052)	-0.010	(0.045)	-0.114	(0.052)*	-0.100	(0.055)
Not living with mother	-0.180	(0.052)**	-0.181	(0.049)**	-0.058	(0.062)	-0.083	(0.064)
Number of siblings	0.008	(0.012)	0.009	(0.013)	0.006	(0.018)	0.000	(0.018)
Independent school			0.111	(0.335)				
Secondary modern school	-0.013	(0.088)	-0.015	(0.093)	-0.113	(0.104)	-0.150	(0.101)
Grammar/selective school	-0.257	(0.126)*	-0.157	(0.194)				
Had careers classes	0.166	(0.050)**	0.015	(0.048)	0.035	(0.051)	0.019	(0.052)
Had own careers interview	0.165	(0.045)**	0.172	(0.047)**	0.166	(0.048)**	0.163	(0.049)**
Had work experience in Year 11	0.062	(0.059)	0.022	(0.061)	0.034	(0.060)	0.048	(0.061)
Average class size	0.003	(0.009)	0.007	(0.009)	0.021	(0.009)*	0.020	(0.010)*
% eligible for free school meals	-0.056	(0.165)	-0.224	(0.157)	0.149	(0.210)	0.123	(0.216)
% SEN with statement	-1.857	(1.176)	-0.026	(0.079)	-2.026	(1.374)	-1.914	(1.362)
% SEN without statement	-0.232	(0.188)	-0.121	(0.140)	0.203	(0.261)	0.192	(0.268)
Identified as having SEN							-0.004	(0.077)
Received a statement of SEN							-0.063	(0.083)
Previously been in residential or foster care							0.033	(0.111)
Parents always/frequently attended parents' evenings							-0.008	(0.050)
Parents read to children every night or often							-0.079	(0.046)
Frequent parental help with examination options, etc							0.097	(0.045)*
Observations	868		779		632		607	

Table A4.10
Determinants of obtaining at least Level 2 via vocational qualifications among low-achieving former truants
Data source: Youth Cohort Study
Robust standard errors are shown in parentheses
* = Coefficient significant at 5%   ** = Coefficient significant at 1%

Variable	Cohort 8		Cohort 9		Cohort 10		Cohort 10	
Female	0.061	(0.030)*	0.110	(0.041)**	0.051	(0.037)	0.043	(0.038)
Black	0.091	(0.097)	-0.177	(0.130)	0.169	(0.128)	0.152	(0.136)
Asian	0.092	(0.072)	0.096	(0.096)	-0.032	(0.081)	0.006	(0.088)
Other ethnic group	0.085	(0.121)	-0.056	(0.164)	0.099	(0.174)	0.052	(0.173)
Senior occupation father	0.011	(0.040)	0.052	(0.055)	0.024	(0.046)	0.021	(0.047)
Father's occupation missing	-0.013	(0.041)	-0.006	(0.054)	-0.035	(0.048)	-0.023	(0.050)
Senior occupation mother	0.023	(0.043)	0.058	(0.063)	0.052	(0.055)	0.053	(0.057)
Mother's occupation missing	-0.087	(0.037)*	0.090	(0.054)	0.072	(0.049)	0.074	(0.051)
Live in privately owned home	0.065	(0.034)	0.069	(0.048)	0.118	(0.040)**	0.102	(0.042)*
Live with both parents in later sweep	0.086	(0.042)*	0.101	(0.058)	0.033	(0.049)	0.036	(0.051)
Live with father only in later sweep	0.119	(0.096)	-0.025	(0.102)	-0.017	(0.077)	-0.011	(0.079)
Live with mother only in later sweep	0.064	(0.055)	0.212	(0.073)**	0.070	(0.067)	0.090	(0.070)
Number of siblings	-0.004	(0.010)	0.006	(0.013)	0.014	(0.017)	0.016	(0.017)
Had careers classes	0.041	(0.048)	0.052	(0.060)	0.021	(0.047)	0.012	(0.048)
Had own careers interview	0.078	(0.045)	0.124	(0.070)	0.028	(0.055)	0.021	(0.056)
Had work experience in Year 11	0.135	(0.055)*	0.099	(0.082)	0.055	(0.064)	0.078	(0.065)
Identified as having SEN							0.010	(0.071)
Received a statement of SEN							-0.159	(0.064)*
Previously been in residential or foster care							0.131	(0.127)
Parents always/frequently attended parents' evenings							0.107	(0.043)*
Parents read to children every night or often							-0.013	(0.040)
Frequent parental help with examination options, etc							0.047	(0.041)
Observations	1,229		645		745		719	

Table A4.11
Determinants of obtaining at least Level 2 via vocational qualifications among low-achieving former serious truants
Data source: Youth Cohort Study
Robust standard errors are shown in parentheses
* = Coefficient significant at 5%   ** = Coefficient significant at 1%

Variable	Cohort 8		Cohort 9		Cohort 10		Cohort 10	
Female	0.054	(0.057)	0.075	(0.074)	0.047	(0.064)	0.038	(0.065)
Black	0.082	(0.176)	−0.115	(0.190)	0.066	(0.239)	−0.111	(0.171)
Asian	0.046	(0.148)	0.407	(0.158)*	−0.120	(0.099)	−0.073	(0.113)
Other ethnic group	−0.008	(0.200)			−0.042	(0.254)	−0.056	(0.243)
Senior occupation father	−0.027	(0.088)	0.122	(0.108)	0.124	(0.087)	0.101	(0.094)
Father's occupation missing	−0.035	(0.070)	−0.023	(0.097)	−0.041	(0.081)	−0.032	(0.083)
Senior occupation mother	0.044	(0.091)	0.092	(0.112)	−0.016	(0.085)	0.008	(0.091)
Mother's occupation missing	−0.098	(0.063)	0.206	(0.111)	0.263	(0.090)**	0.289	(0.097)**
Live in privately owned home	0.038	(0.059)	0.087	(0.079)	0.187	(0.062)**	0.191	(0.064)**
Live with both parents in later sweep	0.113	(0.072)	0.161	(0.103)	0.039	(0.078)	0.040	(0.081)
Live with father only in later sweep	0.235	(0.161)	0.006	(0.169)	−0.014	(0.127)	0.019	(0.135)
Live with mother only in later sweep	0.103	(0.094)	0.132	(0.140)	0.022	(0.137)	0.058	(0.146)
Number of siblings	0.002	(0.017)	−0.013	(0.025)	0.016	(0.025)	0.024	(0.026)
Had careers classes	0.149	(0.078)	0.109	(0.097)	0.019	(0.082)	−0.012	(0.087)
Had own careers interview	0.114	(0.072)	−0.036	(0.129)	−0.031	(0.087)	−0.062	(0.090)
Had work experience in Year 11	0.149	(0.084)	0.103	(0.113)	−0.025	(0.093)	0.008	(0.093)
Identified as having SEN							−0.036	(0.103)
Received a statement of SEN							−0.176	(0.074)*
Previously been in residential or foster care							0.292	(0.217)
Parents always/frequently attended parents' evenings							0.119	(0.067)
Parents read to children every night or often							−0.025	(0.072)
Frequent parental help with examination options, etc							0.022	(0.070)
Observations	352		191		235		223	

5 The relationship between vocational qualifications and labour market outcomes

Introduction

This chapter examines what happens to the previously disengaged individuals after they have completed their education and moved on to the labour market. The previous chapter showed that this group of pupils can re-engage in learning, enter further education and obtain vocational qualifications. The aim of this chapter is to present analyses that show the impact such vocational qualifications can have on such individuals' labour market outcomes.

As discussed in the Introduction in Chapter 1, it is necessary at this point to introduce a new data set, given that the data sets used so far either do not follow individuals into the labour market (PLASC/NPD) or they observe individuals in the labour market for only a very short period of time (YCS). Therefore the Labour Force Survey (LFS) is used for the remainder of the analysis, since the primary aim of this data set is the documentation of people's working lives. The downside is that the LFS does not contain information on individuals' time at school, and so our previous indicator of disengagement (truancy) is no longer available. Indeed, the only variables available in the LFS related to time spent in school are the products of that time, namely qualifications obtained. Thus school qualifications, or more precisely the lack of good school qualifications, is taken as an indicator of possible disengagement.

It was shown above that truancy behaviour is associated with a lower success rate at GCSE on average. Thus the lack of GCSE success variable will at least be correlated with the indicator of disengagement used previously, namely truancy. Again it must be stressed, however, that not all of those who fail to obtain good GCSEs were disengaged at school, and there could be many other reasons why their exam results are low. It may therefore be better not to refer to the group without good school qualifications as the previously disengaged at all, but simply as low school achievers, and to see what impact the acquisition of vocational qualifications has on this group, in the knowledge that it will contain, among others, most of the formerly disengaged pupils identified earlier.

Following a brief literature review, the next section presents the LFS data in more detail, describing the qualification and labour market status variables available. This is followed by a discussion of the results and some conclusions.

Literature review

As in the previous chapters, the review presented here is in no way intended to be a comprehensive audit of all the work in this area, but merely a brief description of some recent work in the field.

Two studies provide evidence about the impact further participation in learning has on the labour market outcomes of the previously disengaged and disaffected. The word 'previously' implies that the further learning might change this, but both studies report that the training was not of a sufficient level to lift these people out of a cycle of low-paid employment and unemployment. It is also pertinent that both studies report that these people were disaffected with schooling, and not education (also reported by Attwood *et al.* 2004a, 2004b). These are both small-scale, regional studies, but the findings are similar, despite one being carried out in Scotland and the other in north-east England.

Furlong and Cartmel (2004) conducted in-depth interviews with 32 young men, all of whom had experienced five years or more of being unemployed. It found that those with low levels of skills and qualifications go in and out of employment on short-term contracts, usually working for agencies for low wages. Those few who were able to escape this cycle had left school with somewhat better qualifications and had received moral and material support and encouragement from their family. These young men were not work shy, and nor were they hostile to the idea of training or education. However, the training they received had little, if any, impact on their employment records. The researchers noted: 'Our evidence also suggests that government-sponsored training programmes rarely provide disadvantaged young men with the sort of skills that would facilitate secure entry into the more desirable sectors of the labour market' (p27).

Webster *et al.* (2004) interviewed 34 young adults 'several years' after they had been interviewed for a previous study. They lived in very deprived wards in the north-east of England and worked in jobs that were 'insecure, low-paid, unskilled and lacking in prospects' (p41). Despite 'dispiriting experiences of school', these people had re-engaged with formal learning and in general enjoyed the experience, especially the social opportunities and personal satisfaction. However, they were of short duration and they were basic and 'had not helped them move to secure employment' (p35).

For example ... poor and casualised local labour market opportunities meant that individuals were placed in New Deal options that they did not want, were short-lived, were of poor quality and provided little long-term benefit in terms of future occupation. They did not enhance educational opportunities for the less well qualified and led to low-waged, unrewarding and insecure employment. (p41)

Cyclical movement around the labour market, unemployment and short-term or sometimes unfinished education and training courses remained the norm. (p35)

The analyses to be presented in this chapter offer slightly more optimistic results about the possibility of improving labour market outcomes for the previously disengaged. However, the focus here will be on formal qualification acquisition and not just any periods of training.

The analysis to be conducted here extends that undertaken by McIntosh (2004). In that paper, the impact of vocational qualifications on the labour market outcomes, in particular the wages and employment likelihoods, of individuals with no or low-level qualifications from school were analysed. The results suggested that vocational qualifications obtained by this group could raise the probability of employment by as much as academic, school-based qualifications at the same level. Vocational qualifications can also raise the wages of unqualified school-leavers, though in this case not by as much as academic, school qualifications at the same level. The current analysis updates this paper in three ways, by:

- using the most recent data available, from the 2004 Labour Force Survey

- considering a wider range of labour market outcomes, thus providing more information about the type of jobs open to individuals who re-engage and obtain qualifications in further education

- considering individual qualifications and not just qualification levels.

The next section now describes this data set and the relevant variables that it contains in more detail.

Data set and the variables

The Labour Force Survey

The LFS is a nationally representative, quarterly survey, interviewing about 120,000 individuals in around 60,000 British households. Respondents remain in the LFS for five consecutive quarters, after which they are replaced by a new incoming group. The data set used here merges the information from the four quarters of 2004 into a single annual data set for that year. To ensure that no individual appears twice in the annual data set, while at the same time making the sample size as large as possible, only individuals being surveyed for the first and last time (their first and fifth wave interviews) were included. Such sample selection has the added attraction that individuals are only asked about their earnings the first and last times that they appear in the LFS.

Further restrictions were placed on the data set to be used in the analysis. First, the sample was restricted to those in their twenties. As discussed above, the aim of the analyses in this chapter is to examine the impact of vocational qualification acquisition on the labour market outcomes of those who left school with no or only low-level qualifications. These impacts are likely to have changed considerably over time, given that the nature of both the education system and the labour market have also changed greatly over time, such that in earlier years unqualified school-leavers had access to unskilled manual work without the need for any qualifications, whereas such unskilled jobs are disappearing for today's young people, and so the impact of vocational qualifications on obtaining employment is likely to be greater for them. Given that one of the objectives of this study is to provide some evidence on the usefulness of various paths for today's young people after leaving school, evidence obtained from data on recent school-leavers will clearly be of more use than evidence based on the data of people who left school many years ago.

The upper age limit of 29 is therefore put in place to keep the study relevant to current young people. The lower age limit of 21 was chosen, rather than, for example, 16, to give individuals time to have acquired vocational qualifications after leaving school, and also time for those qualifications to have begun to have an impact on their labour market outcomes. The latter is necessary, because individuals do not find jobs immediately, and it may take some time before they obtain a job for which the skills learned on their course can be used, and so earn a return.

The second restriction placed on the sample is that only British-born individuals are included. The reason for this is that the sample is to be subdivided according to the level of qualifications obtained in (British) schools. Just because immigrants have no qualifications from British schools does not, of course, mean that they are unqualified or have low qualifications, and thus their presence in the group defined as lacking British qualifications could seriously affect the results. To avoid such problems, only British-born respondents to the LFS are considered.

Indicators of school attainment

With the detailed information on qualifications available in the LFS, six levels of attainment in terms of school qualification achieved can be identified, namely those who:

- report no school-level qualifications
- obtain some GCSEs but fail to obtain any at Grade C
- obtain at least one GCSE at Grade C or above but fail to obtain five such qualifications
- acquire five or more GCSEs at Grades A*–C
- obtain one A-level
- obtain two or more A-levels.

For the analysis that follows, however, the number of these groups is reduced from six to four, because of the lower number of individuals to be found in the 'GCSE D–G' and the 'one A-level' categories causing concerns about cell sizes. The four groups are therefore:

- no school qualifications
- the GCSE D–G
- one to four GCSE A*–C groups combined (labelled low-level lower secondary qualifications)
- the five or more GCSE A*–C group (labelled high-level lower secondary qualifications), and the one A-level and the two or more A-levels combined (labelled upper secondary qualifications).

The focus of the analysis will be on the first group, who left school with no qualifications, with the results presented for the other groups to contrast their labour market outcomes with those of the unqualified school-leavers.

Labour market variables

Given the nature of the LFS, a lot of information is available about individuals' labour market activities. The first factor that we focus on here is whether individuals are actually in work or not. For those who are in work, various indicators are studied which should demonstrate the quality of that job, namely:

- its full-time/part-time status
- its permanent/temporary status
- the tenure of the worker in that job
- the actual job that is being done (occupation)
- the wage received.

The next section contains the results of such an analysis.

Results

The distribution of the sample by highest school qualification

The starting point of this section is to consider how many of our sample of individuals in their twenties fall into each of the school attainment categories. This is illustrated in Table 5.1 and Figure 5.1.

Table 5.1

Percentage of pupils at each level of school qualification, by gender
Data source: Labour Force Survey

School qualifications	Males	Females
None	20.2	16.7
Low-level lower secondary	24.0	22.1
High-level lower secondary	18.3	20.2
Upper secondary	37.5	41.0

These results illustrate that the key group of interest here, those who report no school qualifications at all, represent 20% of the male twenty-something sample and 17% of the female sub-sample.[37] They therefore represent a minority – but a significant minority – of the full population. The remaining figures in the table show that female pupils' small advantage in terms of attainment continues throughout the distribution, with, for example, 20% obtaining five or more good GCSEs compared to 18% of male pupils, and 41% obtaining at least one A-level, compared to 37.5% of male pupils.

37
Although such figures are somewhat higher than official sources, responses to the question asking for the age at which the respondent completed full-time education reveal that the vast majority (86%) of the unqualified school-leavers left education by the age of 17 (and most of these by the age of 16). It therefore would appear that the over-supply of numbers in the unqualified group are not graduates simply not bothering to report school qualifications to the LFS (though they are instructed to report all qualifications), which would have had serious consequences for the analysis of this group. The over-supply, however, seems more likely to be caused by individuals who obtain only one or two low-grade GCSEs not reporting these, which obviously has less serious implications for the analysis of the unqualified group.

Figure 5.1
Percentage of pupils at each level of school qualification, by gender
Data source: Labour Force Survey

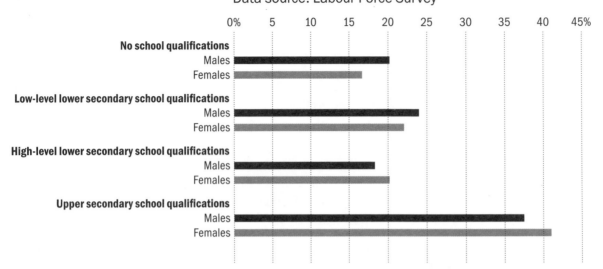

Key points

■ A significant minority of young people continue to leave school with no qualifications.

■ The achievement of girls is slightly better than that of boys.

Qualifications obtained after leaving school

Before examining the labour market outcomes for individuals with and without vocational qualifications, it would be of interest to examine how many actually obtain further qualifications, by level of school attainment, so that if any advantages of vocational qualifications are observed, it will be clear how many gain these advantages. Table 5.2 therefore shows the proportion reaching each level of attainment in terms of post-school qualifications (where the levels are defined as vocational Level 1 qualifications, vocational Level 2 qualifications, vocational Level 3 qualifications and higher level – higher education and high-level vocational – qualifications), separately for each level of school attainment.

Table 5.2
Percentage obtaining post-school qualifications,
by highest level of school qualifications
Data source: Labour Force Survey

	Males	Females
No school qualifications		
+ none	50.3	57.7
+ vocational Level 1	18.4	14.8
+ vocational Level 2	14.9	11.9
+ vocational Level 3	10.6	8.0
+ above Level 3	5.8	7.6
Low-grade lower secondary qualifications		
+ none	27.7	29.0
+ vocational Level 1	18.6	19.8
+ vocational Level 2	26.0	24.8
+ vocational Level 3	20.7	19.1
+ above Level 3	7.0	7.4
High-grade lower secondary qualifications		
+ none	25.7	22.7
+ vocational Level 1	12.0	15.0
+ vocational Level 2	14.7	17.1
+ vocational Level 3	24.6	24.4
+ above Level 3	23.0	20.9
Upper secondary qualifications		
+ none	23.8	19.9
+ vocational Level 1	7.6	6.4
+ vocational Level 2	2.6	2.7
+ vocational Level 3	4.9	5.9
+ above Level 3	61.1	65.0

The results above show that over half (50.3% of males and 57.7% of females) of those who failed to obtain any qualifications at school have also failed to acquire any post-school qualifications by the time they are in their twenties. One of the objectives of this research study has been to examine whether further education can provide a second chance to the previously disengaged young people, but the numbers presented here suggest that only a limited number of the group in question are pursuing this option. Of those who do acquire qualifications post-school, the level most frequently acquired is only Level 1. Only about 30% of those who left school with no qualifications subsequently manage to reach Level 2 via vocational qualifications, and only about 16% reach Level 3.

In contrast, Table 5.2 also shows that those individuals who did acquire qualifications at school are more likely to obtain further qualifications after leaving school. Only around a quarter of those who obtained at best GCSEs at school do not acquire any more qualifications subsequently, while this figure for those who obtained A-levels at school is again around a quarter for males and about 20% for females.

For each of the three groups who acquired qualifications at school, the most common level subsequently reached is one level above their school qualifications. Thus those who obtained low-level GCSEs at school are most likely to obtain a Level 2 qualification subsequently, while those who obtained five or more good GCSEs at school are most likely to acquire a Level 3 qualification in further education. Finally, those who obtained A-levels at school are overwhelmingly most likely to obtain a high-level qualification (most commonly a degree) during their post-compulsory education.

Key points

■ The majority of both young men and women who get no qualifications at school also do not obtain any qualifications after school.

■ If they acquire post-school qualifications, they are most likely to be at Level 1. Only one in three manage to reach Level 2, and one in six reach Level 3.

■ Individuals who did acquire qualifications at school are also more likely to also obtain qualifications after leaving school, most typically at one level above their highest school qualification.

The relationship between qualifications and employment likelihood

This section presents the analysis of the impact of qualification acquisition on labour market outcomes, starting with the likelihood of being in a job. For each of the labour market aspects being considered, the analysis will be the same, essentially looking at the impact of the interaction between school and post-school qualifications. In this way the impact of vocational qualifications on labour market outcomes can be examined, and assessment made as to whether these impacts vary according to the attainment level that individuals achieved at school. In each case, the raw, average value of the labour market characteristic for each level of attainment is presented first, followed by regression coefficients, which control for the impact of other variables that can influence the characteristic.

Table 5.3 shows the employment rates[38] for each of the qualification interactions. Considering first males in their twenties, the first set of figures shows that the acquisition of vocational qualifications is strongly associated with the likelihood of being in work for unqualified school-leavers. Thus, among this group of men, if they have not acquired any qualifications after school, and so remain completely unqualified, then only two-thirds (67%) are employed at the time of the survey. However, this employment rate rises quite quickly as different levels of attainment via vocational qualifications are achieved. Thus, among unqualified male school-leavers in their twenties, the employment rate is 78% for those who achieve Level 1 vocational qualifications, 87% for Level 2 and 95% for Level 3.[39] Once employment rates are up in the nineties, or close to them, there is little to worry about for that group, since employment is never going to be 100% due to normal turnover in the labour market. Thus even if young men leave school with no qualifications at all, their employment rate can nevertheless be similar to their qualified fellow school-leavers, if they acquire vocational qualifications after leaving school, at least at Level 2.

38
In this case, the employment rate includes both employees and the self-employed.

39
The employment rate drops back slightly to 90% among the few unqualified male school-leavers who acquire HE qualifications, but this is mainly because more of them are still in full-time education in their twenties. In addition, there are so few in this group that the precision of any estimates derived for them will be reduced somewhat.

Table 5.3
Employment rates, by qualification combinations
Data source: Labour Force Survey

	Males	Females
No school qualifications		
+ none	67.0	32.8
+ vocational Level 1	78.3	50.8
+ vocational Level 2	87.0	59.2
+ vocational Level 3	94.9	83.5
+ above Level 3	89.8	91.3
Low-grade lower secondary qualifications		
+ none	85.8	54.5
+ vocational Level 1	82.9	65.2
+ vocational Level 2	88.4	70.2
+ vocational Level 3	89.8	80.1
+ above Level 3	92.0	88.5
High-grade lower secondary qualifications		
+ none	89.5	68.3
+ vocational Level 1	92.8	77.1
+ vocational Level 2	90.1	77.5
+ vocational Level 3	96.0	87.5
+ above Level 3	96.7	93.8
Upper secondary qualifications		
+ none	90.6	82.5
+ vocational Level 1	94.4	87.9
+ vocational Level 2	94.0	84.0
+ vocational Level 3	93.7	86.9
+ above Level 3	93.0	92.0

One obvious question to ask at this stage is the causality between employment status and vocational qualification acquisition. The interpretation that paints the best picture for vocational qualifications is that it is precisely their acquisition that has led to their holders finding work. An alternative interpretation, however, implying the reverse causality, is that those already in work are more likely to have access to workplace training that could lead to the acquisition of vocational qualifications.

The earlier paper by McIntosh (2004), considering the same relationship as here for an earlier time period, considered these possibilities, using the longitudinal element of the LFS where the same individuals are surveyed for five quarters in a row. The results showed that, while it is true that many vocational qualifications are obtained by people already in work, it is also true that considering only those not in work at a particular point in time, those who acquire vocational qualifications before the time they are next surveyed (three months later) are more likely to have moved into employment than those who have not acquired any qualifications.

Another possibility is that vocational qualification acquisition and employment do not directly affect each other, but are affected by another variable, causing the apparent relationship between them. For example, more motivated or ambitious individuals may be more likely to acquire further qualifications and to find employment, thus explaining why when one is observed, the other is likely to be too. McIntosh (2004) also investigated this possibility, but found that allowing for unobserved individual characteristics, such as motivation, did not affect the results at all.[40] Thus it seems that, even if it does not explain all of the relationship between employment likelihood and vocational qualification acquisition, at least some of the positive association between the two is due to a causal effect of qualification acquisition on employment, and so vocational qualifications are having the beneficial effects for unqualified school-leavers being implied in the discussion above. These further investigations will not be repeated here again on the 2004 data set.

40
This was done by including a fixed effect for each individual in a panel data model, which was intended to pick up unobserved characteristics of individuals that are constant over time.

Looking at the males who left school with some qualifications, the beneficial effects of vocational qualifications are smaller. This is essentially because their school qualifications already give them a high employment rate, and so there is little room for post-school qualifications to have a further effect. For example, even looking at the lowest group of qualified school-leavers, 86% of those men who acquired some GCSEs but failed to reach the five or more benchmark are in work at the time of the survey, even if they have not acquired any further qualifications after school. Among those who do get further qualifications, the employment rate rises only to 88% for Level 2 qualifications, and to 90% for Level 3 qualifications (and is actually lower for Level 1 qualifications). There are similarly small correlations between vocational qualifications and the employment prospects of men with higher levels of school achievement, for the same reason that their employment rates are already very high.

For women, very large differences in employment rates are observed according to level of vocational qualification acquired, made possible because employment rates without further qualifications are lower, particularly for lower qualified school-leavers. Thus women who leave school with no qualifications, and then fail to acquire any post-school qualifications, have only a 33% chance of employment by the time they are in their twenties. The majority of such women are thus out of work, most being classified as inactive in the labour market rather than unemployed. Among those who have acquired a vocational qualification at Level 1, however, 51% are in employment, which rises again to 59% and 84% for Level 2 and Level 3 qualifications respectively. Thus moving across the vocational qualification levels, employment rates change from being very low to as high as those of well-qualified school-leavers.

Unlike for men, the acquisition of vocational qualifications in women is associated with higher employment rates among those who left school with some qualifications, and not just the unqualified school-leavers. Thus women with GCSEs, but fewer than five at Grades A*–C, have an employment rate of 55% if they have no subsequent qualifications, but 65%, 70% and 80% if they acquire vocational qualifications at Levels 1, 2 and 3 respectively. Even for those women who left school with five or more good GCSEs, those with vocational qualifications are still significantly more likely to be employed than those without. It is only for women who acquired qualifications at the end of upper secondary schooling that the acquisition of vocational qualifications is not associated with a higher employment rate.

41
The results for these control variables are not shown in the tables, for reasons of space.

Table A5.1 in the Regression Appendix shows the results of a regression analysis of employment rates, which allow controls for other factors, such as age, ethnicity and region of residence, to be included.[41] As in some of the previous analyses in earlier chapters, the dependent variable (whether employed or not) is again a dichotomous, yes/no variable, and so a probit equation is estimated to take account of this. The coefficients and their standard errors are shown in the table, with asterisks used to denote statistical significance. Next to these, in square brackets, are the numbers of most interest, namely the marginal effects, which show the change in the probability of employment associated with the acquisition of each qualification.

The first thing to notice about Table A5.1 is that all of the coefficients are statistically significant at the 1% level. Thus all of the groups indicated have a significantly higher likelihood of being employed than the reference group, who are the completely unqualified, either from school or post-school. Thus for men, if they leave school with no qualifications, they are 4.4 percentage points more likely to be employed when aged in their twenties if they have acquired a vocational qualification at Level 1. If they have acquired a vocational qualification at Level 2, they are 7.8 percentage points more likely to be employed than the totally unqualified, while the effect for a Level 3 vocational qualification is 9.9 percentage points. It is interesting that the latter two effects are similar to those associated with academic school qualifications at these two levels (which are 8.9 percentage points for five or more GCSEs, high-grade lower secondary qualifications – ie Level 2 – and 9.2 percentage points for A-levels, upper secondary qualifications, ie Level 3). Thus, at least in terms of finding a job, unqualified male school-leavers can close the probability gap on their former colleagues who achieved success at school, if they acquire vocational qualifications after leaving school. Further analyses will show whether jobs being obtained are actually of the same quality for the two groups who have reached Level 2 or 3 via the academic and vocational routes.

Finally for men, Table A5.1 confirms that for the group who have at best low-grade lower secondary qualifications, there is a slightly higher employment likelihood associated with vocational qualification acquisition at Levels 2 and 3. For men with five or more good GCSEs or A-levels, there is very little impact of vocational qualifications on their employment likelihood, and they remain about 10 percentage points more likely to be in employment than the completely unqualified, whatever level of vocational qualifications they hold.

For women, as expected, the marginal effects reported in Table A5.1 are much larger, given the low employment likelihood of the unqualified group. Thus, for women who left school with no qualifications, if they subsequently acquire a vocational qualification at Level 1, they are 11.4 percentage points more likely to be employed in their twenties than those who have remained unqualified. Similarly, women who reach Level 2 or 3 via vocational qualifications are 15 and 20.3 percentage points, respectively, more likely to be employed than the totally unqualified. These last two probability differences are again similar to, though slightly less than, the change in the likelihood of employment if Level 2 or 3 qualifications are reached via the academic route of school qualifications (five or more good GCSEs with an 18.1 percentage point effect, and A-levels with a 21.5 percentage point effect).

Finally, Table A5.1 shows that vocational qualification acquisition is more strongly associated with employment for qualified school-leavers among women rather than among men. Thus women who leave school with some GCSEs, but fewer than five Grade A*–Cs, are 13.2 percentage points more likely to be employed in their twenties than those women who did not achieve any qualifications at school. If the former group then go on to acquire more qualifications after leaving school, their employment probability gap over the totally unqualified rises to 16.9 percentage points at Level 1, 18.8 percentage points at Level 2 and 20.8 percentage points at Level 3. There is a similar increase in employment probability, though smaller in size, for women with five or more good GCSEs as they acquire vocational qualifications. Only women who left school with A-levels do not see any benefit of vocational qualifications for their employment probability, which remains at about 20 percentage points higher than that of the totally unqualified, whatever the former group's vocational qualification acquisition (though the gap does increase dramatically to 37 percentage points when the A-level group acquire an HE qualification).

Key points

- For unqualified school-leavers, the acquisition of vocational qualifications is strongly associated with higher employment rates.

- For men, a vocational qualification at Level 2 or 3 virtually closes the employment probability gap relative to those who reached these levels via school-based academic qualifications (five or more good GCSEs and A-levels respectively), while for women the gap is closed considerably.

- For men, there is little change in the probability of employment with vocational qualification acquisition among any group who acquired qualifications at school. For women, employment likelihoods continue to rise with vocational qualification acquisition, albeit at a falling rate, for levels of school achievement all the way up to, and including the five or more GCSE Grade A*–C group. Only those women who achieved A-levels at school do not see any benefit in acquiring vocational qualifications, in terms of their employment likelihood.

Qualifications and full-time/part-time status

The previous section focused on how the employment rate varies by the level of qualification achieved. From this point onwards, the analysis focuses on the type of employment secured by those in work. Since a number of the characteristics are not strictly relevant to self-employed workers, such as the wage rate or the temporary/permanent nature of the job, only employees are considered. The first job characteristic to be studied is the full-time/part-time status of the job. The rates of part-time work, by qualification level, are displayed in Table 5.4. As usual, the results are presented separately for men and women, with this division being particularly important in this case, given the large difference in working on a part-time basis between the sexes.

Table 5.4
Part-time employment rates among employees,
by qualification combinations
Data source: Labour Force Survey

	Males	Females
No school qualifications		
+ none	6.2	45.9
+ vocational Level 1	8.8	36.0
+ vocational Level 2	1.8	40.6
+ vocational Level 3	1.5	30.5
+ above Level 3	3.2	6.7
Low-grade lower secondary qualifications		
+ none	5.8	44.6
+ vocational Level 1	4.6	31.5
+ vocational Level 2	4.6	34.3
+ vocational Level 3	2.0	25.5
+ above Level 3	8.5	23.7
High-grade lower secondary qualifications		
+ none	5.9	24.0
+ vocational Level 1	3.0	18.6
+ vocational Level 2	4.2	27.6
+ vocational Level 3	3.4	20.5
+ above Level 3	5.9	20.4
Upper secondary qualifications		
+ none	7.1	20.9
+ vocational Level 1	4.8	15.4
+ vocational Level 2	5.9	20.7
+ vocational Level 3	3.7	22.3
+ above Level 3	4.2	9.9

The results reveal that the likelihood of finding a part-time or full-time job is not strongly related to the acquisition of qualifications. For men, there is some suggestion that within each school qualification grouping, the rate of part-time working falls with the acquisition of post-school qualifications up to and including Level 3, after which there is a slight increase in the rate again for those with HE qualifications. Given the small numbers of men who work in part-time jobs, however, probably not too much attention should be paid to these small differences.

Many more women, of course, work in part-time jobs. Table 5.4 shows that it is the completely unqualified, either from school or post-school, that have the highest part-time rate (46%). However, there is little evidence of a consistent pattern across the levels of post-school qualifications, and so there is no evidence that, for example, the acquisition of vocational qualifications helps individuals avoid part-time work. This may be to be expected, given that the availability of part-time work is not necessarily an indicator of a lower quality job, and could in fact be a desirable characteristic that is obtained by individuals with more bargaining power (ie a higher level of qualifications) in the labour market.

Table A5.2 contains the results from a multivariate analysis of the incidence of part-time working. The column for males, with a lack of statistical significance on all coefficients except one, and the marginal effects consistently being fewer than 3 percentage points, confirms the suggestion from the raw data above, that there is very little variation in the likelihood of part-time working, across qualification categories.

For females, most of the estimated coefficients are statistically significant and many are large in terms of their marginal effects, with almost all greater than 10 percentage points. However, these are all measured relative to the omitted category of the totally unqualified, revealing that, among women, all qualification groups are significantly less likely to work part-time than the unqualified. Once any qualifications have been obtained, however, there is no consistent pattern as to whether further qualification attainment will raise or lower the likelihood of working part-time.

Key points

■ Among men, there is no evidence of any statistically significant relationship between qualification acquisition and the likelihood of working part-time. This is principally due to the fact that, overall, only small numbers of men work in part-time jobs.

■ Many more women work in part-time jobs, and the evidence suggests that those with no qualifications at all are most likely to perform such jobs. Beyond that, however, among those young women with some qualifications, there is little evidence of a systematic relationship between further qualification acquisition and the likelihood of working part-time.

Qualifications and permanent/temporary status

The next indicator of job quality to be considered is whether it is a permanent job, or temporary in some way, for example due to being only seasonal work or the existence of a fixed-term contract. Table 5.5 displays the rate of temporary working among employees holding the various qualifications as their highest qualifications.

As with the part-time results, there is little evidence for any relationship between the acquisition of qualifications and the permanent/temporary nature of jobs. Certainly it cannot be said that higher qualifications are more likely to 'win' for individuals a permanent contract. Indeed, among men, within each school attainment grouping, the highest rate of temporary working is to be found among those who have gone on to acquire HE qualifications. This finding may be a result of the types of jobs taken by HE graduates; a subsequent section will consider the occupations of individuals with differing qualifications.

Similar results are obtained for women, in the sense that there is again little discernable pattern in temporary working across qualification groups, and that within all school attainment levels, except one in this case, the highest rate of temporary working is among those women who have acquired HE qualifications. There is no consistent difference in the rate of temporary employment at given qualification levels between men and women.

Table 5.5
Temporary employment rates among employees,
by qualification combinations
Data source: Labour Force Survey

	Males	Females
No school qualifications		
+ none	4.9	2.4
+ vocational Level 1	9.0	6.4
+ vocational Level 2	3.0	3.7
+ vocational Level 3	4.9	2.4
+ above Level 3	13.4	9.7
Low-grade lower secondary qualifications		
+ none	3.7	3.6
+ vocational Level 1	3.6	5.6
+ vocational Level 2	3.9	4.4
+ vocational Level 3	3.2	4.2
+ above Level 3	7.3	6.5
High-grade lower secondary qualifications		
+ none	3.1	2.6
+ vocational Level 1	2.1	5.7
+ vocational Level 2	4.9	1.7
+ vocational Level 3	1.8	4.0
+ above Level 3	6.1	5.0
Upper secondary qualifications		
+ none	7.4	6.4
+ vocational Level 1	4.7	4.1
+ vocational Level 2	1.9	1.6
+ vocational Level 3	2.0	4.5
+ above Level 3	9.6	11.0

Table A5.3 contains the results of the multivariate analysis. They confirm the absence of any real relationship between qualifications attainment and the permanent/temporary status of jobs. The most regular pattern occurs among women, for whom the rate of temporary employment among those with HE qualifications is statistically significantly higher in three of the four school qualification groups, and almost significant in the fourth. Perhaps surprisingly, therefore, it seems that those with the highest qualifications are actually the most likely to work in temporary jobs.

Key points

■ There is little evidence for a relationship between individuals' qualifications and their likelihood of working in a job that is temporary for some reason.

■ The strongest association is a positive one between the acquisition of HE qualifications and the probability of one's job being temporary in some way.

Qualifications and months of tenure

The previous section considered whether individuals' jobs were open-ended or had a fixed completion date, and whether jobs were likely to finish earlier in the future for individuals with particular qualifications. The information in the LFS also allows an examination of the data to see how long an individual has been working for a current employer at the time of the survey. Such measures of current tenure, measured in months, are reported in Table 5.6.

Once again, it is very difficult to observe any particular pattern in the results. In most school attainment/gender cells in the table, the longest tenure is observed among those who have reached Level 3 via vocational qualifications. However, the next level of qualifications, HE qualifications, are typically associated with the shortest current tenure. The latter result is consistent with the greater likelihood of temporary employment among this group, as observed above. The most likely explanation, however, is that, given that the sample respondents are aged 21 to 29, those who acquired an HE qualification may have only recently completed their courses, and so will have spent less time in their current job than those who did not attend higher education. The multivariate results controlling for other possible factors in Table A5.4 support the assertion that there is no pattern in the tenure rates across qualification groups and few statistically significant findings are obtained, with the exception of shorter tenure for those with HE qualifications, for the reason just suggested above.

Table 5.6
Months of tenure with current employer among employees, by qualification combinations
Data source: Labour Force Survey

	Males	Females
No school qualifications		
+ none	40.0	31.8
+ vocational Level 1	33.4	35.5
+ vocational Level 2	46.1	33.8
+ vocational Level 3	46.0	47.9
+ above Level 3	31.6	27.8
Low-grade lower secondary qualifications		
+ none	41.6	35.0
+ vocational Level 1	37.4	35.5
+ vocational Level 2	41.4	39.2
+ vocational Level 3	45.8	42.3
+ above Level 3	33.1	35.2
High-grade lower secondary qualifications		
+ none	38.6	39.3
+ vocational Level 1	40.1	40.9
+ vocational Level 2	39.0	40.5
+ vocational Level 3	45.0	39.2
+ above Level 3	42.6	35.1
Upper secondary qualifications		
+ none	34.7	35.8
+ vocational Level 1	33.2	39.1
+ vocational Level 2	38.5	41.9
+ vocational Level 3	42.0	37.7
+ above Level 3	29.3	27.3

> **Key points**
>
> ■ There is no relationship between qualifications acquired and months of tenure in current job, with the exception of shorter tenure among those with HE qualifications, for the simple reason that they will have spent less time on the labour market.

Qualifications and occupations

This section considers the types of job performed by people with different qualifications. Type of job is identified by aggregated, one-digit occupation codes.[42] It would have been of interest to examine more disaggregated occupations at the two- or even three-digit level, but the number of observations in the school qualification/post-school qualification gender cells were not sufficient to allow this level of disaggregation. Thus type of job falls into one of the nine categories used in the one-digit Standard Occupational Classification. These occupations are arranged broadly in a hierarchical order, so that more senior occupations are towards the top. The proportions of people at each qualification level in each occupation are recorded in Tables 5.7 and 5.8, separately for males and females.

Beginning with men who left school with no qualifications, and who have not acquired qualifications after leaving school, Table 5.7 shows that the majority are in low-level occupations. In particular, 53% are in either elementary occupations or unskilled/semi-skilled manual occupations. Outside these two occupation groups, such men are most likely to be in skilled manual jobs. No other job class employs more than 10% of unqualified men.

Moving across the columns, it can be seen to what extent the acquisition of vocational qualifications changes this occupational distribution. The table shows that it can have quite a large effect. Vocational qualifications at Level 1 do not change the distribution too much, with actually a slight increase in the proportion in the lowest two occupation groups. Once individuals reach Level 2 via vocational qualifications, however, they are definitely less likely to be found in low-level occupations, with the major change being a fall in the number in elementary occupations. Most move to skilled trades occupations, which now employs almost 45% of this group of men. Moving on to Level 3 merely reinforces this trend, with the proportion in the lowest two occupations falling further to just 20%, again caused primarily by a fall in the number in elementary occupations. Skilled trades jobs are again the major beneficiary, with this job class now employing over half of all unqualified male school-leavers who acquire Level 3 vocational qualifications. In addition, associate professional occupations have now increased their share to 11%. Finally, among the small number of men who leave school unqualified but nevertheless go on to acquire an HE qualification, there is a large shift in occupation structure, with the HE qualification allowing such men to largely leave manual jobs behind and move into the senior non-manual occupations, with the top three occupation categories (managers, professionals and associate professionals) employing just over 70% of this admittedly small group of men.

42
The Standard Occupational Classification (SOC) classifies occupations according to a hierarchical series of codes. The one-digit level is the broadest classification of occupations, with each job being assigned to one of the digits from one to nine (1: managers and senior officials, 2: professional occupations, 3: associate professional and technical occupations, 4: administrative and secretarial occupations, 5: skilled trade occupations, 6: personal service occupations, 7: sales and customer service occupations, 8: process, plant and machine operatives and 9: elementary occupations. As more digits are added, jobs are defined in more detail, for example, 10: general managers, 11: production managers, etc).

Table 5.7
Occupation structure among employees,
by qualification combinations, males
Data source: Labour Force Survey

	+ none	+ vocational Level 1	+ vocational Level 2	+ vocational Level 3	+ above Level 3
No school qualifications					
Managers and senior officials	3.93	3.92	3.71	3.52	14.21
Professional occupations	1.23	1.63	2.32	0.00	28.24
Associate professional and technical	5.15	6.91	6.88	11.32	28.12
Administrative and secretarial	4.06	5.32	2.33	4.55	3.35
Skilled trades occupations	23.38	13.86	44.73	50.17	9.46
Personal service occupations	2.32	3.52	1.04	4.81	2.65
Sales and customer service occupations	7.06	5.82	4.85	5.29	9.62
Process, plant and machine operatives	18.85	32.84	18.70	14.40	0.00
Elementary occupations	34.03	26.19	15.43	5.95	4.34
Low-grade lower secondary qualifications					
Managers and senior officials	4.96	7.88	5.49	7.77	8.71
Professional occupations	1.44	1.18	2.37	4.37	14.28
Associate professional and technical	6.63	6.51	6.89	10.03	31.03
Administrative and secretarial	10.08	7.12	6.60	6.62	10.80
Skilled trades occupations	20.97	18.48	36.57	44.45	8.80
Personal service occupations	1.76	1.14	2.80	2.54	3.93
Sales and customer service occupations	10.43	6.41	7.43	6.35	8.19
Process, plant and machine operatives	19.18	29.48	14.08	9.38	4.58
Elementary occupations	24.55	21.80	17.77	8.49	9.69
High-grade lower secondary qualifications					
Managers and senior officials	14.35	14.76	5.11	13.03	16.48
Professional occupations	1.47	5.32	3.25	5.15	22.32
Associate professional and technical	12.87	28.32	12.54	18.09	27.32
Administrative and secretarial	13.97	6.98	7.74	6.74	7.98
Skilled trades occupations	12.61	10.72	39.10	29.79	11.88
Personal service occupations	2.33	2.31	0.52	2.64	0.73
Sales and customer service occupations	13.79	4.01	8.68	6.67	5.75
Process, plant and machine operatives	11.16	15.12	12.72	7.38	1.75
Elementary occupations	17.44	12.46	10.35	10.52	5.79
Upper secondary qualifications					
Managers and senior officials	12.96	13.69	10.56	14.82	14.07
Professional occupations	6.58	7.01	8.06	7.48	33.36
Associate professional and technical	21.04	30.60	23.11	19.13	26.70
Administrative and secretarial	17.49	18.05	14.16	23.48	10.78
Skilled trades occupations	5.97	3.97	23.03	15.28	3.09
Personal service occupations	1.17	2.23	6.24	1.21	1.28
Sales and customer service occupations	17.21	8.13	7.89	7.34	5.67
Process, plant and machine operatives	4.25	5.17	0.00	3.96	1.37
Elementary occupations	13.33	11.16	6.94	7.30	3.69

Table 5.8
Occupation structure among employees,
by qualification combinations, females
Data source: Labour Force Survey

	+ none	+ vocational Level 1	+ vocational Level 2	+ vocational Level 3	+ above Level 3
No school qualifications					
Managers and senior officials	6.88	9.18	8.12	6.51	13.27
Professional occupations	0.00	3.66	0.00	3.28	17.65
Associate professional and technical	6.58	1.74	5.51	6.56	26.04
Administrative and secretarial	17.15	17.18	20.13	25.33	17.10
Skilled trades occupations	1.69	4.11	0.00	2.69	2.29
Personal service occupations	16.11	25.03	33.67	38.71	14.73
Sales and customer service occupations	21.27	17.23	15.70	7.71	2.43
Process, plant and machine operatives	4.93	4.13	2.11	2.11	1.26
Elementary occupations	25.40	17.74	14.76	7.11	5.22
Low-grade lower secondary qualifications					
Managers and senior officials	6.37	8.99	4.66	9.07	6.76
Professional occupations	0.00	0.90	1.58	0.36	5.87
Associate professional and technical	6.42	5.22	6.33	10.20	23.54
Administrative and secretarial	26.72	33.24	25.84	23.80	13.95
Skilled trades occupations	1.83	2.17	1.17	2.43	1.15
Personal service occupations	13.59	23.58	30.06	33.00	30.39
Sales and customer service occupations	24.65	14.36	19.20	12.80	10.60
Process, plant and machine operatives	3.47	3.01	2.31	2.89	1.75
Elementary occupations	16.96	8.53	8.85	5.45	5.98
High-grade lower secondary qualifications					
Managers and senior officials	9.59	6.96	8.87	12.97	7.21
Professional occupations	0.44	2.38	3.68	3.12	9.12
Associate professional and technical	7.48	11.89	8.40	10.97	39.57
Administrative and secretarial	36.38	39.40	30.69	30.71	17.09
Skilled trades occupations	1.78	0.43	2.70	1.21	0.97
Personal service occupations	9.98	13.06	21.54	23.71	13.05
Sales and customer service occupations	20.93	16.08	14.58	10.36	9.65
Process, plant and machine operatives	3.87	1.31	1.27	0.71	0.80
Elementary occupations	9.54	8.47	8.26	6.23	2.53
Upper secondary qualifications					
Managers and senior officials	9.44	13.25	8.84	11.49	9.93
Professional occupations	4.10	5.84	0.00	3.42	30.80
Associate professional and technical	17.09	20.98	14.73	16.63	28.95
Administrative and secretarial	35.73	33.10	36.35	31.44	16.56
Skilled trades occupations	0.65	0.72	5.16	1.60	0.46
Personal service occupations	9.54	11.11	16.88	18.00	5.34
Sales and customer service occupations	17.05	6.33	7.34	10.54	5.96
Process, plant and machine operatives	1.26	0.00	1.38	0.00	0.31
Elementary occupations	5.15	8.68	9.32	6.89	1.69

The pattern of occupational shift with the acquisition of post-school qualifications is very similar for those with some, but fewer than five, good GCSEs, as it was for the unqualified males. The main difference is the starting position, with a lower proportion (44%) to be found in the lowest two occupation categories when no post-school qualifications are held, and a higher proportion to be found in junior non-manual occupations such as administrative (10%) and sales (10%). The effect of vocational qualification acquisition is the same as before, however, with a decline in the numbers working in low-grade occupations (down as low as 18% if Level 3 vocational qualifications are acquired) and a growth in the numbers working in skilled manual jobs (up to 44% if Level 3 vocational qualifications are acquired). Again, 10% of the Level 3 vocational qualification group work in associate professional jobs, but the real breakthrough into senior non-manual jobs only really occurs when HE qualifications are acquired.

The relationship between vocational qualification acquisition and occupation structure is much weaker for men who left school with five or more good GCSEs, or with A-levels. Thus there is some movement into senior non-manual occupations as vocational qualifications are acquired, but significant numbers (29% of those with good GCSEs and 41% of those with A-levels) were already in such occupations with no post-school qualifications acquired.

In comparison with men, in Table 5.8, fewer unqualified women school-leavers work in the lowest two occupation groupings, primarily because of the small numbers of women working in unskilled manual jobs (though similar numbers work in elementary occupations). Instead, unqualified women are more likely to be found in administrative, personal service and sales occupations, relative to their male counterparts. The acquisition of vocational qualifications by previously unqualified women is then associated with a re-distribution of this group between the four dominant occupation classes, with a reduction in the number working in elementary occupations and sales occupations, and a rise in the number working in administrative and personal service occupations. There is absolutely no movement at all into other occupation groups which continue to attract small numbers of these women, unlike for men, where a big increase in the proportion working in skilled manual occupations was noted. As was found for men, the small number of unqualified female school-leavers who nevertheless go on to acquire an HE qualification do see a large change in occupation structure, with the majority (57%) now working in senior non-manual positions.

For women who leave school with some GCSEs, but fewer than five, the same four occupational groupings (administrative, personal service, sales and elementary occupations) dominate again. The difference relative to the unqualified school-leavers is that more of the low GCSE group are initially employed in administrative jobs, even with no post-school qualifications, and this number does not change much as vocational qualifications are acquired in the post-school period. Thus the only occupational grouping that increases in number with vocational qualification acquisition for this group of low-GCSE women is personal services.

Very similar patterns are observed for women who left school with either five or more good GCSEs or A-levels. Among both of these groups, the occupation group with the highest number of such women is the administrative group, and much smaller numbers than the similarly qualified male school-leavers are observed in the senior non-manual occupations (17% of those with five or more good GCSEs and 31% of those with A-levels). As for men, there is very little movement into these top occupations as vocational qualifications are acquired by well-qualified female school-leavers, and indeed the whole occupation structure for these groups of women is barely affected by the acquisition of vocational qualifications. Only when HE qualifications are acquired can large numbers of these women in senior occupations be seen.

The multivariate analysis in this section simply considers whether an individual works in the lowest two occupations or not. Thus the dependent variable in these equations is a simple yes/no variable, and so a probit equation is employed, as before. The results are contained in Table A5.5 in the Regression Appendix. As expected, almost all of the estimated coefficients are negative and statistically significant, showing that the totally unqualified (who form the reference category) are the most likely to work in the two lowest occupation classes.

Focusing in particular first on unqualified male school-leavers, the results show that a vocational qualification at Level 1 does not have any impact on their probability of working in a low-grade job, but vocational qualifications at Levels 2 and 3 do reduce the probability of their working in such jobs, by 11 and 16 percentage points respectively. For those men who left school with some, but fewer than five, good GCSEs, the impact of vocational qualifications post-school also does not become apparent until Level 2, but once they do, they reduce the probability of working in a low-grade occupation by 12 and 18 percentage points at Levels 2 and 3 respectively. For those young men who left school with five or more good GCSEs or A-levels, they are less likely to work in low-grade occupations than their unqualified counterparts, and the acquisition of vocational qualifications does not affect this advantage they hold (with the possible exception of Level 3 vocational qualifications for the five or more GCSE group). It is only the acquisition of HE qualifications that further reduces the chances of these groups working in the lowest ranked occupations.

For women, the first thing to notice is that the marginal effects are much lower than the equivalents in the male column. Thus, although the totally unqualified are again the most likely to work in low-grade occupations among women, the difference in their likelihood of doing so and that of their qualified counterparts is smaller for women than for men. Put another way, the influence of qualifications on moving people up the occupation hierarchy is smaller for women than for men. In particular, the acquisition of vocational qualifications has only very small effects on reducing the probability of working in the lowest ranked occupations for women, with the largest of these small effects being for women who left school with no qualifications.

Key points

■ The acquisition of post-school vocational qualifications is associated with unqualified male school-leavers moving up the occupation hierarchy from elementary and unskilled/semi-skilled manual occupations into skilled manual occupations. Only if they acquire an HE qualification, however, do these men break into senior non-manual occupations in significant numbers.

■ Similar effects are observed for men who leave school with fewer than five good GCSEs, while for those with good school-leaving qualifications, significant numbers work in senior occupations even when they hold no post-school qualifications, and so the influence of vocational qualifications on the occupation structure of such individuals is smaller.

■ Unqualified female school-leavers are most likely to work in administrative, personal service, sales and elementary occupations. As they acquire vocational qualifications, they move away from the latter two occupation groups, and into the former two. Unlike for men, very few move into skilled manual jobs.

■ Similar patterns are observed for women who left school with some, but fewer than five, good GCSEs, with the exception that higher numbers with no post-school qualifications work in administrative occupations, but this proportion does not change as post-school vocational qualifications are acquired.

■ For women who leave school with five or more good GCSEs or with A-levels, the acquisition of post-school vocational qualifications has virtually no impact on their occupation structure, and it is only HE qualifications that get such women into senior non-manual occupations.

Qualifications and earnings

The final job characteristic to be considered here is the one that perhaps people care about most, namely how much they earn in their job. Table 5.9 shows the average hourly wage for the various combinations of school and post-school qualifications. The analysis is restricted to full-time workers only, to mitigate against the effects of individuals with different qualifications being more likely to work part-time, given that part-time workers are known to earn less per hour than full-time workers.

The estimates of the average wages across qualification groups show some instability, in that they do not always demonstrate a continuous increase as qualification level rises. This may reflect a lack of precision in the wage estimates, caused by a smaller sample size since not all respondents divulge their wages.

What is clear, and as expected, is that the totally unqualified have the lowest hourly wage rate for both men and women. Considering men first, if those who left school with no qualifications subsequently acquire vocational qualifications, then their average wage rises appropriately (and in this case monotonically with the level of the vocational qualification). For men who acquired some, but fewer than five, good GCSEs, vocational qualifications do not have much impact on their wages until a Level 3 qualification is acquired, while men with five or more good GCSEs or with A-levels do not receive any wage return to any vocational qualification at any level,[43] and only benefit from HE qualifications.

43
With the exception of the suspiciously large average wage for men with five or more good GCSEs and a Level 1 vocational qualification, which could be one of the statistical anomalies referred to above.

Table 5.9
Average hourly wages among full-time employees,
by qualification combinations
Data source: Labour Force Survey

	Males	Females
No school qualifications		
+ none	6.73	6.16
+ vocational Level 1	7.34	6.15
+ vocational Level 2	7.79	7.78
+ vocational Level 3	8.19	6.72
+ above Level 3	10.79	10.14
Low-grade lower secondary qualifications		
+ none	7.37	6.75
+ vocational Level 1	7.38	6.98
+ vocational Level 2	7.53	6.58
+ vocational Level 3	8.31	6.70
+ above Level 3	9.80	7.51
High-grade lower secondary qualifications		
+ none	7.79	6.87
+ vocational Level 1	9.22	8.23
+ vocational Level 2	8.62	7.29
+ vocational Level 3	8.79	7.74
+ above Level 3	10.29	8.68
Upper secondary qualifications		
+ none	9.46	7.74
+ vocational Level 1	9.68	8.84
+ vocational Level 2	9.73	7.97
+ vocational Level 3	8.58	7.77
+ above Level 3	12.12	10.55

It is of interest that the acquisition of a vocational qualification by previously unqualified male school-leavers raises their wages to £7.79 per hour on average, exactly the same as the average wage of men with five or more good GCSEs from school but no subsequent qualifications. It therefore appears that for men who did not acquire any qualifications at school, perhaps because they were disengaged, vocational qualifications to Level 2 offer a second chance, allowing those men to earn as much on the labour market as they would have done if they had obtained five or more good GCSEs (ie reached Level 2) at school. At Level 3, this effect is not observed, however, and a previously unqualified man acquiring a Level 3 vocational qualification still earns less than a man who achieved A-levels at school (£8.19 versus £9.46 per hour).

The pattern of results for women are not as stable as for men. There is still some evidence, however, that similar to the effect for males, vocational qualifications can raise the wages of women who left school with no qualifications, although unlike the case for men, this effect for women does not start until Level 2. The more erratic nature of the results for women is shown by the fact that the average wage for Level 2 vocational qualifications is greater than that for Level 3 vocational qualifications, among the unqualified school-leavers.

There is little evidence that vocational qualifications raise the wages of women who fall into any of the three groupings where school qualifications were obtained (although, as for men, there is a large effect of Level 1 vocational qualifications for those who left school with five or more good GCSEs, which is difficult to explain). Finally, in Table 5.9, it is worth noting that the average wage among unqualified female school-leavers who subsequently acquire a Level 2 vocational qualification (£7.78) is actually greater than the average wage among women who reached Level 2 via the academic route and achieved five or more good GCSEs at school (£6.87). At Level 3, however, the vocational qualification cannot match the wage achieved by those with A-levels from school (£6.72 versus £7.74).

Table A5.6 in the Regression Appendix contains the determinants of wages in a multivariate setting. The dependent variable in these equations is actually the natural logarithm of hourly earnings, so that the estimated coefficients in Table A5.6 should be interpreted as proportional changes in wages if a particular qualification is held. There are also some differences to the control variables in these wage equations, compared to the multivariate equations estimated above. First, potential labour market experience, measured as current age minus age when completed full-time education, is used instead of age, since those individuals who have achieved higher qualifications will have spent longer in education, have less labour market experience, and so earn less for this reason, which is something that needs to be controlled for.[44] Also, controls for sector (public or private) and workplace size, both of which are known to influence wages, are added to the specifications used to investigate other labour market characteristics above.

[44] It would have been preferable to control for actual labour market experience rather than potential labour market experience, but such information is not available in the LFS.

The results, as usual, are quite consistent with the raw averages presented above. Thus there is a strong monotonic relationship between vocational qualification acquisition and wages for those who left school with no qualifications. These wage returns mean that previously unqualified school-leavers who reach Level 2 via vocational qualifications now earn as much on average as those with five or more good GCSEs, though the returns to a Level 3 vocational qualification still lag behind the returns to A-levels. In addition – and again as in the raw data – vocational qualifications have less impact on the wages of those who did acquire qualifications at school, although there is probably more evidence for some beneficial effects of vocational qualifications on the wages of those who got five or more good GCSEs at school in the multivariate equation controlling for other determinants of wages than was found in the raw data, particularly for men.

Key points

■ Vocational qualifications have a significant impact on the wages of those who left school with no qualifications, but little impact on the wages of those who did acquire qualifications at school.

■ A Level 2 vocational qualification raises the wages of a previously unqualified school-leaver to the level received by an individual with Level 2 GCSEs from school. The wage return attached to a Level 3 vocational qualification, however, cannot match that attached to acquiring A-levels at school.

Labour market outcomes and particular qualifications

So far throughout the discussion of the results, labour market outcomes have been attributed to the level of qualifications obtained, rather than particular qualifications. Studying all individuals at a given level of qualification provided more observations for estimating the labour market impacts, which was important given that the sample size was already reduced because of the focus on only British-born individuals in their twenties. This section briefly considers the association between labour market outcomes and particular qualifications. Because of the focus of this research, only vocational qualifications will be considered here. In addition, results are reported only for employment likelihoods, low-grade occupation employment likelihoods and wages, since these seemed to be the key labour market characteristics that can vary with the qualifications held by individuals. The sample is restricted to those who left school with no qualifications, since they are the main focus of this study, and the results are displayed in Table A5.7 and A5.8 in the Regression Appendix for males and females respectively.

Looking first at the results for males, the two most successful qualifications, in that they score a statistically significant impact in each of the three columns, are NVQs at Level 2 and completed apprenticeships, both of which increase the chances of previously unqualified male school-leavers being in work, avoiding the lowest two occupation categories and earning a higher wage. In fact, these are the only two qualifications to attract a statistically significant positive coefficient in the wage equation, though as the sample size is now very small at just 438 observations, this will increase standard errors and make it more difficult to observe statistically significant effects. A couple of other qualifications, while not having a statistically significant impact on earnings, still successfully raise the probability of the holder being in employment and avoiding the lowest ranked occupations, namely Advanced Craft City and Guilds qualifications, and NVQs at Level 3 and above. It therefore appears that it is the more practical vocational qualifications, rather than the more theoretical ones, that benefit previously unqualified male school-leavers.

45
Some of the cells in the table are blank, meaning that the qualification in question was perfectly related to the dependent variable and so no coefficient could be estimated. For example, for the women in the sample with a teaching qualification, none were out of work and none were working in either of the two lowest classed occupations.

For women in Table A5.8,[45] no qualification successfully affects all three labour market outcomes, primarily again as a result of the very small sample for the wage equations meaning few statistically significant effects are observed in that equation. The most successful qualifications for previously unqualified female school-leavers are certainly the NVQs, which at Level 3 significantly raise the probability of employment and significantly reduce the probability of working in a low-ranked occupation, with their positive wage effect just failing to achieve statistical significance. Also at Level 2, NVQs significantly raise the probability of being employed and also the wage received, while their negative impact on the probability of working in a low-grade occupation is almost statistically significant. Apprenticeship appears to be less important for women than for men, although it does still increase their chances of employment.

Key points

■ Looking at the individual qualifications rather than simply qualification levels, the qualifications that have the largest impact on labour market outcomes (improving employability, occupational status and wages) for both men and women seem to be NVQs (though not at Level 1). In addition, apprenticeships and City and Guilds qualifications at Advanced Craft level seem to have an impact for men only.

Conclusion

This chapter has looked at the relationship between qualifications acquired after leaving school and labour market outcomes, focusing on vocational qualifications obtained in further education. The results are positive as far as those who left school with no qualifications are concerned.

First, and perhaps most importantly, the acquisition of vocational qualifications is positively associated with the probability of being in work. Furthermore, individuals who left school with no qualifications but subsequently obtain a Level 2 vocational qualification are just as likely to be in employment as those who obtained five or more good GCSEs at school. The same applies for Level 3 vocational qualifications and A-levels. Vocational qualifications are therefore successful in reducing the gap in employability between those who have acquired qualifications at school and those who have not.

Of course, it is one thing to have a job, and another thing to have a good-quality job, and so the analyses continued by considering a range of other characteristics of the jobs being done by people with different levels of qualifications.

The results showed that the incidence of part-time work, temporary jobs and months of tenure in current job do not vary systematically with qualification attainment. The positive interpretation of this statistically insignificant result is that those previously unqualified individuals who acquire vocational qualifications and then find a job are not more likely to end up in low-quality (part-time if involuntary, temporary or short-term jobs) than individuals who have already reached Level 2 or 3 through their school qualifications.

In terms of the jobs actually being performed, unqualified workers are most likely to be found in elementary or unskilled occupations. There is evidence that for individuals who left school with no qualifications, acquiring vocational qualifications after school will reduce the likelihood of their working in such occupations, with the likelihood decreasing as the level of vocational qualification achieved increases. Previously unqualified men are most likely to move into skilled manual jobs on acquisition of vocational qualifications, while previously unqualified women are most likely to move into administrative or personal service occupations on acquisition of vocational qualifications.

Finally, in terms of wages, for the group who left school with no qualifications, the evidence suggests that the acquisition of vocational qualifications after school is associated with the receipt of higher wages. Indeed, the results suggest that a previously unqualified individual who acquires a vocational qualification at Level 2 earns as much, on average, as an individual who reached Level 2 via the academic route through obtaining five or more good GCSEs. At Level 3, however, the wages of a previously unqualified individual with a vocational qualification cannot match the wages of an individual with A-levels.

Overall, therefore, the evidence suggests that the acquisition of vocational qualifications can be beneficial for individuals who have failed at school but re-entered education in further education, in terms of better labour market prospects, particularly greater employability, higher job status and higher earnings. It should be remembered that this evidence is cross-sectional, and therefore means that the acquisition of vocational qualifications is shown to be associated with these good outcomes, rather than proved to be directly causing them. Nevertheless, to the extent that causality can be inferred to explain at least some of the cross-sectional correlation, this suggests that gaining vocational qualifications can reduce some of the harmful effects of remaining unqualified. The challenge is therefore to increase the number of low-achievers from school re-entering education (or training) and acquiring such qualifications, since the evidence in Table 5.2 showed that only a minority of those without any school qualifications currently obtain qualifications after leaving school.

Regression appendix

Table A5.1
Multivariate analysis of the factors associated with being in work
Data source: Labour Force Survey
Robust standard errors are shown in parentheses
Marginal effects are shown in square brackets
Equations also control for region of residence, age and ethnicity
The omitted categories are 'No school qualifications'
and 'No post-school qualifications'
* = Coefficient significant at 5%   ** = Coefficient significant at 1%

	Males			Females		
No school qualifications						
+ vocational Level 1	0.295	(0.098)**	[0.044]	0.485	(0.100)**	[0.114]
+ vocational Level 2	0.671	(0.115)**	[0.078]	0.718	(0.110)**	[0.150]
+ vocational Level 3	1.203	(0.171)**	[0.099]	1.398	(0.149)**	[0.203]
+ above Level 3	0.876	(0.213)**	[0.086]	1.897	(0.200)**	[0.215]
Low-grade lower secondary qualifications						
+ none	0.598	(0.086)**	[0.075]	0.572	(0.072)**	[0.132]
+ vocational Level 1	0.496	(0.096)**	[0.065]	0.839	(0.083)**	[0.169]
+ vocational Level 2	0.750	(0.091)**	[0.086]	0.993	(0.077)**	[0.188]
+ vocational Level 3	0.757	(0.102)**	[0.085]	1.285	(0.091)**	[0.208]
+ above Level 3	0.981	(0.180)	[0.091]	1.632	(0.150)**	[0.212]
High-grade lower secondary qualifications						
+ none	0.839	(0.105)**	[0.089]	0.948	(0.083)**	[0.181]
+ vocational Level 1	1.001	(0.159)**	[0.093]	1.171	(0.100)**	[0.196]
+ vocational Level 2	0.825	(0.131)**	[0.086]	1.234	(0.095)**	[0.202]
+ vocational Level 3	1.257	(0.134)**	[0.105]	1.567	(0.093)**	[0.225]
+ above Level 3	1.373	(0.150)**	[0.107]	2.009	(0.116)**	[0.236]
Upper secondary qualifications						
+ none	0.878	(0.102)**	[0.092]	1.398	(0.091)**	[0.215]
+ vocational Level 1	1.096	(0.164)**	[0.096]	1.671	(0.134)**	[0.215]
+ vocational Level 2	1.144	(0.291)**	[0.095]	1.424	(0.184)**	[0.202]
+ vocational Level 3	1.122	(0.199)**	[0.095]	1.585	(0.134)**	[0.212]
+ above Level 3	1.020	(0.070)**	[0.128]	1.907	(0.064)**	[0.370]
Observations	6,851			7,608		

Table A5.2
Multivariate analysis of the factors associated with being in a part-time job
Data source: Labour Force Survey
Robust standard errors are shown in parentheses
Marginal effects are shown in square brackets
Equations also control for region of residence, age and ethnicity
The omitted categories are 'No school qualifications'
and 'No post-school qualifications'
* = Coefficient significant at 5%   ** = Coefficient significant at 1%

	Males			Females		
No school qualifications						
+ vocational Level 1	0.219	(0.162)	[0.022]	-0.267	(0.152)	[-0.066]
+ vocational Level 2	-0.481	(0.259)	[-0.027]	-0.156	(0.154)	[-0.041]
+ vocational Level 3	-0.564	(0.298)	[-0.029]	-0.447	(0.163)**	[-0.102]
+ above Level 3	-0.260	(0.354)	[-0.017]	-1.328	(0.227)**	[-0.190]
Low-grade lower secondary qualifications						
+ none	0.031	(0.147)	[0.003]	-0.046	(0.110)	[-0.013]
+ vocational Level 1	-0.081	(0.166)	[-0.006]	-0.433	(0.119)**	[-0.101]
+ vocational Level 2	-0.136	(0.154)	[-0.010]	-0.295	(0.108)**	[-0.073]
+ vocational Level 3	-0.517	(0.213)*	[-0.029]	-0.587	(0.116)**	[-0.127]
+ above Level 3	0.224	(0.217)	[0.023]	-0.658	(0.158)**	[-0.135]
High-grade lower secondary qualifications						
+ none	-0.050	(0.161)	[-0.004]	-0.582	(0.118)**	[-0.126]
+ vocational Level 1	-0.286	(0.241)	[-0.019]	-0.843	(0.137)**	[-0.159]
+ vocational Level 2	-0.211	(0.210)	[-0.015]	-0.507	(0.121)**	[-0.114]
+ vocational Level 3	-0.326	(0.178)	[-0.021]	-0.733	(0.113)**	[-0.150]
+ above Level 3	0.007	(0.162)	[0.001]	-0.813	(0.115)**	[-0.159]
Upper secondary qualifications						
+ none	0.016	(0.147)	[0.001]	-0.696	(0.115)**	[-0.144]
+ vocational Level 1	-0.167	(0.217)	[-0.012]	-0.946	(0.150)**	[-0.168]
+ vocational Level 2	-0.009	(0.307)	[-0.001]	-0.708	(0.203)**	[-0.141]
+ vocational Level 3	-0.096	(0.260)	[-0.007]	-0.683	(0.143)**	[-0.139]
+ above Level 3	-0.143	(0.121)	[-0.011]	-1.231	(0.091)**	[-0.283]
Observations	5,428			5,546		

Table A5.3
Multivariate analysis of the factors associated with being in a temporary job
Data source: Labour Force Survey
Robust standard errors are shown in parentheses
Marginal effects are shown in square brackets
Equations also control for region of residence, age and ethnicity
The omitted categories are 'No school qualifications'
and 'No post-school qualifications'
* = Coefficient significant at 5%   ** = Coefficient significant at 1%

	Males			Females		
No school qualifications						
+ vocational Level 1	0.346	(0.166)*	[0.044]	0.443	(0.268)	[0.066]
+ vocational Level 2	-0.178	(0.225)	[-0.015]	0.152	(0.315)	[0.018]
+ vocational Level 3	0.059	(0.221)	[0.006]	0.082	(0.349)	[0.009]
+ above Level 3	0.530	(0.240)*	[0.078]	0.761	(0.263)**	[0.141]
Low-grade lower secondary qualifications						
+ none	-0.078	(0.159)	[-0.007]	0.273	(0.224)	[0.036]
+ vocational Level 1	-0.154	(0.184)	[-0.013]	0.428	(0.226)	[0.062]
+ vocational Level 2	-0.113	(0.161)	[-0.010]	0.306	(0.216)	[0.041]
+ vocational Level 3	-0.104	(0.186)	[-0.009]	0.286	(0.222)	[0.038]
+ above Level 3	0.306	(0.224)	[0.038]	0.625	(0.259)*	[0.106]
High-grade lower secondary qualifications						
+ none	-0.266	(0.189)	[-0.021]	-0.011	(0.247)	[-0.001]
+ vocational Level 1	-0.353	(0.263)	[-0.026]	0.406	(0.235)	[0.059]
+ vocational Level 2	0.045	(0.202)	[0.005]	-0.113	(0.273)	[-0.011]
+ vocational Level 3	-0.434	(0.213)*	[-0.031]	0.289	(0.215)	[0.038]
+ above Level 3	0.212	(0.161)	[0.024]	0.411	(0.214)	[0.059]
Upper secondary qualifications						
+ none	0.191	(0.146)	[0.021]	0.419	(0.206)*	[0.060]
+ vocational Level 1	-0.034	(0.210)	[-0.003]	0.236	(0.251)	[0.030]
+ vocational Level 2	-0.362	(0.434)	[-0.026]	-0.101	(0.450)	[-0.010]
+ vocational Level 3	-0.300	(0.327)	[-0.023]	0.326	(0.260)	[0.045]
+ above Level 3	0.446	(0.117)**	[0.053]	0.855	(0.180)**	[0.119]
Observations	5,429			5,546		

Table A5.4
Multivariate analysis of the factors associated with months of tenure in current job
Data source: Labour Force Survey
Robust standard errors are shown in parentheses
Equations also control for region of residence, age and ethnicity
The omitted categories are 'No school qualifications'
and 'No post-school qualifications'
* = Coefficient significant at 5% ** = Coefficient significant at 1%

	Males		Females	
No school qualifications				
+ vocational Level 1	−9.52	(2.96)**	3.24	(3.90)
+ vocational Level 2	1.52	(3.74)	3.84	(4.03)
+ vocational Level 3	1.86	(4.20)	13.20	(4.38)**
+ above Level 3	−10.69	(5.01)*	−4.47	(3.53)
Low-grade lower secondary qualifications				
+ none	0.46	(2.62)	3.61	(2.93)
+ vocational Level 1	−4.19	(2.87)	2.88	(3.07)
+ vocational Level 2	0.22	(2.69)	7.74	(2.92)**
+ vocational Level 3	3.04	(2.94)	11.30	(3.11)**
+ above Level 3	−11.35	(3.77)**	0.08	(3.64)
High-grade lower secondary qualifications				
+ none	−1.26	(2.80)	8.90	(3.05)**
+ vocational Level 1	−1.06	(3.71)	9.60	(3.26)**
+ vocational Level 2	−2.38	(3.41)	10.68	(3.09)**
+ vocational Level 3	3.72	(2.77)	9.45	(2.80)**
+ above Level 3	−1.11	(2.93)	1.17	(2.79)
Upper secondary qualifications				
+ none	−4.43	(2.47)	6.87	(2.72)*
+ vocational Level 1	−6.54	(3.00)*	6.59	(3.48)
+ vocational Level 2	−1.30	(5.42)	9.73	(4.69)*
+ vocational Level 3	0.56	(3.64)	6.44	(3.42)
+ above Level 3	−15.11	(2.02)**	−6.63	(2.26)**
Observations	5,163		5,354	

Table A5.5
Multivariate analysis of the factors associated with being in an unskilled manual or elementary occupation job
Data source: Labour Force Survey
Robust standard errors are shown in parentheses
Marginal effects are shown in square brackets
Equations also control for region of residence, age and ethnicity
The omitted categories are 'No school qualifications'
and 'No post-school qualifications'
* = Coefficient significant at 5% ** = Coefficient significant at 1%

	Males	Females
No school qualifications		
+ vocational Level 1	0.153 (0.108) [0.045]	-0.262 (0.167) [-0.026]
+ vocational Level 2	-0.495 (0.117)** [-0.110]	-0.503 (0.179)** [-0.041]
+ vocational Level 3	-0.912 (0.145)** [-0.162]	-0.810 (0.208)** [-0.053]
+ above Level 3	-1.727 (0.283)** [-0.198]	-1.008 (0.236)** [-0.057]
Low-grade lower secondary qualifications		
+ none	-0.227 (0.089)* [-0.058]	-0.324 (0.120)** [-0.031]
+ vocational Level 1	-0.064 (0.100) [-0.017]	-0.700 (0.138)** [-0.051]
+ vocational Level 2	-0.555 (0.091)** [-0.123]	-0.731 (0.126)** [-0.054]
+ vocational Level 3	-1.033 (0.108)** [-0.179]	-0.889 (0.139)** [-0.058]
+ above Level 3	-1.230 (0.177)** [-0.184]	-0.908 (0.201)** [-0.056]
High-grade lower secondary qualifications		
+ none	-0.641 (0.102)** [-0.134]	-0.641 (0.132)** [-0.049]
+ vocational Level 1	-0.668 (0.132)** [-0.136]	-0.833 (0.154)** [-0.055]
+ vocational Level 2	-0.819 (0.126)** [-0.154]	-0.860 (0.147)** [-0.056]
+ vocational Level 3	-1.039 (0.106)** [-0.180]	-1.011 (0.135)** [-0.062]
+ above Level 3	-1.534 (0.128)** -[0.209]	-1.413 (0.168)** [-0.069]
Upper secondary qualifications		
+ none	-1.011 (0.101)** [-0.180]	-1.015 (0.140)** [-0.062]
+ vocational Level 1	-1.057 (0.139)** [-0.175]	-0.895 (0.172)** [-0.056]
+ vocational Level 2	-1.466 (0.266)** [-0.191]	-0.649 (0.232)** [-0.048]
+ vocational Level 3	-1.341 (0.188)** [-0.189]	-0.975 (0.181)** [-0.058]
+ above Level 3	-1.705 (0.084)** [-0.316]	-1.560 (0.109)** [-0.145]
Observations	5,429	5,545

Table A5.6
Multivariate analysis of the factors associated with log hourly wages
Data source: Labour Force Survey
Robust standard errors are shown in parentheses
Equations also control for region of residence, potential experience
and its square, ethnicity, public/private sector of work and workplace size
The omitted categories are 'No school qualifications'
and 'No post-school qualifications'
* = Coefficient significant at 5%   ** = Coefficient significant at 1%

	Males		Females	
No school qualifications				
+ vocational Level 1	0.091	(0.039)*	0.043	(0.078)
+ vocational Level 2	0.167	(0.037)**	0.284	(0.084)**
+ vocational Level 3	0.206	(0.042)**	0.092	(0.069)
+ above Level 3	0.459	(0.094)**	0.425	(0.098)**
Low-grade lower secondary qualifications				
+ none	0.071	(0.033)*	0.108	(0.061)
+ vocational Level 1	0.075	(0.035)*	0.146	(0.059)**
+ vocational Level 2	0.115	(0.031)**	0.107	(0.055)
+ vocational Level 3	0.224	(0.033)**	0.150	(0.056)**
+ above Level 3	0.421	(0.053)**	0.266	(0.067)**
High-grade lower secondary qualifications				
+ none	0.158	(0.034)**	0.158	(0.059)**
+ vocational Level 1	0.235	(0.052)**	0.321	(0.060)**
+ vocational Level 2	0.241	(0.039)**	0.194	(0.060)**
+ vocational Level 3	0.298	(0.033)**	0.280	(0.055)**
+ above Level 3	0.496	(0.033)**	0.429	(0.057)**
Upper secondary qualifications				
+ none	0.346	(0.037)**	0.282	(0.059)**
+ vocational Level 1	0.376	(0.046)**	0.364	(0.065)**
+ vocational Level 2	0.393	(0.077)**	0.272	(0.081)**
+ vocational Level 3	0.322	(0.044)**	0.296	(0.061)**
+ above Level 3	0.673	(0.029)**	0.625	(0.054)**
Observations	3,483		3,038	

Table A5.7

Association between key vocational qualifications and selected labour market outcomes, males with no school qualifications

Data source: Labour Force Survey

Robust standard errors are shown in parentheses

The 'In work' and 'In occupation' equations also control for region of residence, age and ethnicity

The 'Wages' equations control for region of residence, potential experience and its square, ethnicity, public/private sector of work and workplace size

+ = Occupation group 8: process, plant and machine operatives; occupation group 9: elementary occupations

* = Coefficient significant at 5% ** = Coefficient significant at 1%

	In work		In occupation groups 8 or 9+		Log hourly wages	
HND/HNC	0.145	(0.443)	-1.370	(0.567)*	-0.289	(0.154)
City and Guilds Advanced Craft level	1.081	(0.525)*	-1.062	(0.462)*	0.062	(0.102)
ONC/OND	0.621	(0.524)	0.154	(0.440)	-0.054	(0.126)
NVQ Levels 3–5	0.836	(0.217)**	-0.734	(0.213)**	-0.009	(0.052)
Complete trade apprenticeship	0.601	(0.151)**	-0.842	(0.170)**	0.259	(0.049)**
City and Guilds Craft level	0.340	(0.399)	1.363	(0.546)*	0.126	(0.133)
BTEC First Diploma/Certificate	0.361	(0.590)	0.181	(0.662)	-0.009	(0.142)
NVQ Level 2/GNVQ Intermediate	0.583	(0.180)**	-0.393	(0.173)*	0.109	(0.050)*
City and Guilds other (Part One)	-0.662	(0.289)*	-0.788	(0.414)	-0.063	(0.100)
RSA Diploma or other	-1.017	(0.480)*			-0.309	(0.081)**
NVQ Level 1/GNVQ Foundation	-0.159	(0.215)	0.403	(0.272)	-0.082	(0.066)
Other qualifications	0.407		0.161		0.061	
Observations	1,256		797		438	

Table A5.8
Association between key vocational qualifications and selected labour market outcomes, females with no school qualifications
Data source: Labour Force Survey
Robust standard errors are shown in parentheses
The 'In work' and 'In occupation' equations also control for region of residence, age and ethnicity
The 'Wages' equations control for region of residence, potential experience and its square, ethnicity, public/private sector of work and workplace size
+ = Occupation group 8: process, plant and machine operatives; occupation group 9: elementary occupations
* = Coefficient significant at 5% ** = Coefficient significant at 1%

	In work		In occupation groups 8 or 9+		Log hourly wages	
Teaching qualification					0.689	(0.127)**
RSA Higher/Advanced Diploma					0.163	(0.123)
Nursing qualification	1.294	(0.653)*			-0.178	(0.692)
HND/HNC	1.109	(0.670)	-0.667	(0.575)	0.126	(0.169)
City and Guilds Advanced Craft level			-0.960	(1.026)	0.087	(0.131)
ONC/OND			-0.242	(0.586)	-0.207	(0.180)
NVQ Levels 3–5	0.918	(0.179)**	-0.699	(0.264)**	0.158	(0.083)
Completed trade apprenticeship	0.989	(0.273)**	-0.557	(0.330)	0.104	(0.117)
City and Guilds Craft level	-0.821	(0.628)	-0.300	(1.007)	-0.322	(0.166)
BTEC First Diploma/Certificate	-0.232	(0.421)			0.246	(0.201)
NVQ Level 2/GNVQ Intermediate	0.387	(0.134)**	-0.358	(0.216)	0.172	(0.065)**
City and Guilds other (Part One)	0.590	(0.345)	0.990	(0.482)*	0.102	(0.146)
RSA Diploma or other	0.310	(0.224)	-0.977	(0.609)	0.171	(0.084)*
NVQ Level 1/GNVQ Foundation	0.437	(0.202)*	0.349	(0.284)	0.004	(0.072)
Other qualifications	0.374		-0.229		0.011	
Observations	1,131		450		281	

** = Occupation group 8: process, plant and machine operatives; occupation group 9: elementary occupations

6 | Conclusions and implications

This study has presented evidence on a number of related issues, including school outcomes, post-compulsory education participation and labour market outcomes, for those who at some point during their school career have been disengaged from their school, education, the learning process, or all three. The analyses conducted have addressed such points as:

■ who the disengaged are

■ what effect their disengagement had on their school examination outcomes

■ how many re-engage with education by participating in post-compulsory education

  ■ what the characteristics are of those who do

  ■ how successful they are in post-compulsory education

  ■ the impact of this participation in continued learning on their labour market outcomes.

Thus the study is a wide-ranging one, which had the intention of telling a continuous story for this group of people from their time at school, through further education and into their working lives.

The indicator of disengagement used in Chapters 3 and 4, examining school and further education, was whether the respondent had played truant at school or not; this could be divided into persistent and occasional truanting, though this distinction made little difference to the results.

At numerous points in this report, it has been stressed that it is not being claimed that truancy is the only way that disengagement can manifest itself, nor that all truants are necessarily completely disengaged from the education process. Rather, this was the variable chosen as the best available indicator of disengagement among existing large, national data sets, which were to form the data source for the analyses undertaken for this study.

The analysis in Chapter 3 revealed that certain characteristics of individuals are associated with truancy behaviour. In particular, it was found that:

■ Girls *report* a higher truancy rate than boys, somewhat surprisingly, given official administrative data that suggests the opposite.

■ After controlling for family background, white pupils have a higher truancy rate than other ethnic groups, although the differences are small.

Family background matters, with the following all more likely to play truant:

■ individuals with one of their parents, especially the mother, missing

■ individuals with parents, particularly the father, in non-professional occupations

■ individuals living in a rented home.

Not surprisingly, school characteristics are important.

■ Pupils in independent and grammar schools report less truancy, relative to comprehensive schools.

■ Within schools, the receipt of careers advice or, in particular, work experience, are associated with a lower probability of playing truant.

Finally, peer groups are important. Whatever an individual pupil's own social background, the higher the proportion of pupils entitled to free school meals in his or her school, the more likely is that individual pupil to play truant himself/herself.

One of the key aims of the report was to look at the impact of such disengagement on outcomes such as exam performance. Chapter 2 had already set the scene on performance using administrative data on pupils throughout their school careers to identify those who under-achieved at Key stages, on the basis of their results at an earlier Key stage. The results suggested that:

■ Girls are less likely to under-achieve than boys.

■ Between Key stages 2 and 3, black pupils are more likely to under-achieve.

■ The ethnic group most likely to under-achieve between Key stages 3 and 4 is white pupils.

One of the implications of the result that girls are less likely to under-achieve is that we further question the finding reported above that girls are more likely to play truant than boys, and it may be safer to conclude that this is a mis-reporting issue among boys.

The pattern of under-achievement by ethnic group is of interest, with black pupils, if they under-achieve, doing so between the ages of 11 and 14, while white pupils under-achieve later, between the ages of 14 and 16. This suggests that teachers and parents should be particularly aware of possible disengagement at these ages, but a clearer understanding is also needed about what is happening in young people's lives to lead to this pattern of under-achievement.

Chapter 2 also showed that, among pupils who under-achieved at Key stage 3, those who then got things back on track and obtained the Key stage 4 results that their Key stage 2 results suggested they should were more likely to be girls and less likely to be boys, and more likely to be Indian, Pakistani, Bangladeshi or Chinese, and less likely to be white pupils. Again, an important question to ask is why white boys, if they have begun to disengage, are less likely to get back on track and re-engage than others.

Finally, this chapter showed, perhaps not surprisingly, that at both Key stages 3 and 4, pupils who receive free school meals (as an indicator of social background) and pupils with special educational needs, are much more likely to under-achieve. A more interesting result is that the free school meals effect is larger for white pupils than for other ethnic groups. Thus, considering all from poorer backgrounds, those from an ethnic group other than white pupils, are less likely to under-achieve than white pupils. Why is it that a poorer background affects those with a white ethnic background more?

Given this scene-setting on under-achievement, a key part of this study links disengagement (as measured by truancy) to under-achievement, in Chapter 4. However, for this part of the analysis, the relative under-achievement measure from the administrative data, defined in terms of the pupil's own past performance, is not available, so the measure used in Chapter 4 is simply whether individuals manage to acquire five or more good GCSEs or not (or at some points, five GCSEs whatever their grade).

The results show that former truants achieve lower GCSE results on average, with the results getting worse as the extent (frequency or regularity) of truancy behaviour increases. However, it is not the case that truancy automatically spells disaster, and a significant proportion of truants still achieve five or more good GCSEs. The analysis shows that it is girls, Asian (relative to both white and black) pupils, those from a more affluent background, those with a secure family and those whose parents take an interest in their education who are more likely to achieve five or more GCSEs at Grades A*–C.

Those who play truant and fail to achieve five or more good GCSEs do, however, have a second chance: they can re-engage in education through further education. The analysis shows that the factors associated with a lower probability of obtaining good GCSEs are the same as those associated with a lower probability of re-engaging – ie white boys, those from a poorer background, those whose parents are less supportive of their education and those not living with both parents. Put together, therefore, these findings on GCSE results and re-engagement suggest the importance of social background, and the need for more support, help and advice for those from more vulnerable backgrounds. This, of course, is not new information, but at least the analysis confirms current thinking.

The final section in Chapter 4 looked at the success of previously disengaged (low-achieving former truants) young people in obtaining qualifications through further education. About half are successful in reaching Level 2 of the National Qualifications Framework through vocational qualifications. However, when the analysis is restricted to very low-achieving former truants (those who fail to achieve five GCSEs at any grade) only 10–15% add any vocational qualifications after school. Among the former (low-achieving) group, the results show that girls, and possibly non-white pupils and those from higher socio-economic backgrounds, are more likely to be successful in this regard. When attention was focused on very low-achieving former truants or serious truants (ie the more seriously disengaged), however, family background had little impact on the likelihood of acquiring vocational qualifications. It therefore seems that individuals' families cannot be relied upon to pull the most seriously disengaged through, and more help and support would need to be given to such people.

The final chapter in the report looked at the impact of the acquisition of vocational qualifications on labour market outcomes, using data from the Labour Force Survey. It was intended to examine the previously disengaged in particular, given the focus of this research project, but no measure of truancy (or any other form of disengagement) was available. Instead, the sample was divided by level of attainment at school, and the analyses focused on those who did not obtain any qualifications at school. The results show that previously unqualified school-leavers who acquire vocational qualifications in further education are more likely to be in work, less likely to be in a low-grade occupation and more likely to earn a higher wage, compared with those who remain unqualified. The change in employment rates and the change in the wage rates (at Level 2 only) compare favourably with the effects of academic qualifications at the same level. Finally, the acquisition of vocational rather than academic qualifications is not more likely to lead to obtaining only part-time, temporary or short-tenured work.

It therefore seems that taking their second chance and re-engaging in further education can be a worthwhile option for those who have previously disengaged. The challenge is therefore to persuade more of them to take up this second chance, since the data in Chapter 5 suggests too few of the unqualified school-leavers are obtaining post-school vocational qualifications at present. The analyses also suggested that the likelihood of vocational qualification acquisition is related to GCSE performance, even among the group of former truants, and that very few of those with fewer than five GCSEs at any grade go on to acquire post-school vocational qualifications.

As this project was designed as a scoping study to see what could be ascertained on the issue of disengagement with large-scale, national data sets, it is important to conclude with some comments on the data. Clearly, the data used in this project has been less than ideal. Truancy is only an indicator of disengagement, as pointed out throughout this report, and more direct questioning about individuals' attitudes to their learning (or even supplementary questions about why individuals were truanting) would allow the disengaged individuals to be identified more accurately.

The analysis – and in particular the definitions used – was not helped by the fact that this was a multi-period analysis, considering individuals in school, in further education and in the labour market. Different data sets have therefore been used at different stages of the analysis, and as such the variables used to indicate the key concepts have changed throughout. For example, truancy was used to identify disengaged learners for most of the report, but then the chapter on the labour market had to use the lack of school qualifications as a (potential) indicator of disengagement. If multi-period research of this kind is to progress – and it is surely of interest to be able to follow individuals through their lives, to determine the full implications of their choices and behaviour at each stage – then more data sets like the birth cohort data sets (the National Child Development Study and the British Cohort Study), which follow people throughout their lives, need to be developed.[46] Alternatively, and this may be the holy grail for researchers, if individuals were given a unique reference number to be used in all administrative and survey data sets, then researchers could link together various data sets using this number, and so track (anonymous) individuals throughout their lives. Whether data protection issues ever allow this to be a reality remains to be seen.

[46] It was considered that these two data sets (containing people born in 1958 and 1970) were too old to be of relevance to the current research.

Finally, some of the contributions made by this study to the literature on disengagement are outlined here. As much of this literature has focused on case study evidence of small numbers of individuals, this research has provided corroborating evidence based on large, national data sets. It has to be admitted, however, that most of the analysis conducted here is focused on individual characteristics such as gender, ethnicity, family background etc, and cannot deal with some of the issues addressed in the case study work, such as motivation, feelings etc. Thus both types of evidence are needed and can help to provide a clearer understanding of the reasons for disengagement and those who are disengaged from secondary education.

The results that stand out from the research presented here as findings of interest that have not been commented on in previous work, and suggest issues for further research, include the following.

- **The age/ethnic group pattern of under-achievement**, whereby under-achievement first takes a hold between the ages of 11 and 14 for black pupils, and between the ages of 14 and 16 for white pupils. An understanding of why this is the case would be useful when developing effective approaches to reduce under-achievement.

- **The free schools meal entitlement/ethnic group pattern of under-achievement**, whereby the negative association between free school meal entitlement and achievement observed among white pupils is much less evident among almost all other ethnic groupings. What is still to be learned, however, is why a poorer social background has less of an effect on pupils from ethnic minority groups than on white pupils.

- **The relationship between seriousness of disengagement and the impact of family background on re-engagement and post-compulsory achievement**. Among low-achieving former truants, family background, socio-economic status and parental interest are related to the likelihood of such young people re-engaging in further education and then being successful in terms of gaining vocational qualification. Thus a good background and supportive family can help many of these people to get their lives back on track. Among more seriously disengaged young people, however (those who truanted on a more regular basis, or who failed to obtain five GCSEs even at Grade G), the impact of such support on re-engagement and success likelihoods seems to disappear. Thus among this group, those from a higher social background or a more supportive family are no more likely to re-engage and/or succeed than those less fortunate than themselves. For the seriously disengaged, therefore, what needs to be ascertained is what additional help and support is required than can be provided by their families.

- **The labour market outcomes for unqualified school-leavers who acquire vocational qualifications post-school**. Although other research studies have looked at the impact of gaining such qualifications on the wage and employment opportunities, the research presented here has looked at a much wider range of outcomes. It has offered some optimistic findings that those previously unqualified young people who acquire vocational qualifications will improve their occupational standing, as well as their wages and employment likelihood. Additionally, they will not be more likely to obtain only part-time, temporary or short-tenure jobs than those who acquired academic qualifications. The question that needs to be addressed, therefore, is how to engage young people who leave school without any qualifications with education via the vocational qualification route, as these qualifications have the potential to deliver greater employability, higher job status and higher earnings to these disengaged young people.

References

Alderson P, Arnold S (1999).
Civil Rights in Schools: school students' views, 1997–1998. Swindon: Economic and Social Research Council.

Attwood G, Croll P, Hamilton J (2004a). Challenging students in further education: themes arising from a study of innovative FE provision for excluded and disaffected young people. *Journal of Further and Higher Education,* 28(1), 107–19.

Attwood G, Croll P, Hamilton J (2004b). Re-engaging with education. *Research Papers in Education,* 18(1), 75–95.

Bricheno P, Younger M (2004).
Some unexpected results of a learning styles intervention? Paper presented at BERA Conference, September 2004, Manchester.

Broadhurst K, Paton H, May-Chaal C (2005). Children missing from school systems: exploring divergent patterns of disengagement in the narrative accounts of parents, carers, children and young people. *British Journal of Sociology of Education,* 26(1), 105–19.

Dalziel D, Henthorne K (2005).
Parents'/Carers' Attitudes Towards School Attendance. Nottingham: DfES Publications.

Deakin Crick R, Taylor M, Tew M, Samuel E, Durant K, Ritchie S (2005). A systematic review of the impact of citizenship education on student learning and achievement. In *Research Evidence in Education Library.* London: EPPI-Centre, Social Science Research Unit, Institute of Education.

Department for Education and Skills (2005). Statistics of Education: the characteristics of low-attaining pupils. *Department for Education and Skills Statistics of Education Series,* 02/05.

Foskett N (2004).
IAG (information, advice and guidance) and young people's participation decisions 14–19. [Working paper]. Nuffield Foundation.
At www.nuffield14-19review.org.uk/files/documents47-1.pdf

Farlie V (2004).
Are apprenticeships any longer a credible vocational route for young people, and can the supply side respond effectively to government policy, and address the needs of learners and employers? [Working Paper 28]. Nuffield Foundation.
At www.nuffield14-19review.org.uk/files/documents52-1.doc

Furlong A, Cartmel F (2004).
Vulnerable young men in fragile labour markets: employment, unemployment and the search for long-term security. York: Joseph Rowntree Foundation.
At www.jrf.org.uk/bookshop/eBooks/1859351808.pdf

Golden S, O'Donnell L, Rudd P (2005).
Evaluation of the Increased Flexibility for 14–16 Year Olds Programme: the second year. Nottingham: DFES Publications.
At www.dfes.gov.uk/research/data/uploadfiles/RR609.pdf

Hoggart L, Smith D I (2004).
Understanding the Impact of Connexions on Young People at Risk. Department for Education and Skills.
At www.dfes.gov.uk/research/data/uploadfiles/RR607.pdf

Kendall S, Cullen M A, White R, Kinder K (2001).
Delivery of the Curriculum to disengaged young people in Scotland. Slough: NFER.
At www.nfer.ac.uk/research-areas/pims-data/summaries/sco-delivery-of-the-curriculum-to-disengaged-young-people-in-scotland.cfm

McCrone T, Morris M (2004).
Research into the Impact of Pre-16 Vocational Education. Slough: NFER.
At http://cep.lse.ac.uk/research/skills/Skills_Publications/McCrone_Morris_2004.pdf

McIntosh S (2004).
The Impact of Vocational Qualifications
on the Labour Market Outcomes
of Low-Achieving School-Leavers.
Centre for Economic Discussion Paper 621.
At http://cep.lse.ac.uk/pubs/download/
dp0621.pdf

Morris M (2004).
*The Case for Careers Education
and Guidance for 14–19 Year Olds.*
Slough: NFER.
At www.nfer.ac.uk/research/downloads/
MM483.doc

Morrision C (2004).
*Support in School the Views of Harder
to Reach Group: additional consultation
exercise gathering the views of
young people, parents/carers who
are 'harder to reach' and agencies
which advocate on their behalf.*
Edinburgh: Scottish Executive
Education Department.
At www.scotland.gov.uk/library5/
education/ssvg-00.asp

Philip K, Shucksmith J, King C (2004).
*Sharing a Laugh? A qualitative study of
mentoring interventions with young people.*
York: Joseph Rowntree Foundation.

Rennison J, Maguire S, Middleton S,
Ashworth K (2005).
*Young People not in Education,
Employment or Training: evidence
from the Education Maintenance
Allowance pilots database.*
Nottingham: DfES Publications.
At www.dfes.gov.uk/research/data/
uploadfiles/RR628.pdf

Salmon G (n–d).
*Working with the Metaphor:
educational therapy as a multidisciplinary
approach to learning difficulties.*
London: Caspari Foundation.
At www.caspari.org.uk/resources/
articles/gs_web.pdf

Schagen I, Benton T, Rutt S (2004).
Study of Attendance in England.
Slough: NFER.

Steedman H, Stoney S (2004).
*Disengagement 14–16: context and
evidence.* CEP Discussion Paper 654.
At http://cep.lse.ac.uk/pubs/download/
dp0654.pdf

Watson J (2004).
*Using Individual Learner Data
to Investigate Progression.*
London: Nuffield Foundation.
At www.nuffield14-19review.org.uk/
files/documents45-1.pdf

Webb R, Vulliamy G (2004).
*A Multi-Agency Approach to Reducing
Disaffection and Exclusion from School.*
Nottingham: DfES Publications.

Webster C, Simpson D, MacDonald R,
Abbas A, Cieslik M, Shildrick T,
Simpson M (2004).
*Poor Transitions: social exclusion
and young adults.* York:
Joseph Rowntree Foundation.
At www.jrf.org.uk/bookshop/eBooks/
1861347340.pdf

Wiseman J (2004).
*Audit of factors affecting participation
and achievement in learning.* Coventry:
Learning and Skills Council.

Appendix

Advisory group and expert seminar – list of participants

Advisory group members

David Andrews, The National Institute for Careers Education and Counselling
Valerie Bayliss, formerly of DfES
Robert Cassen, LSE
Mike Cooper, LSDA
Mick Fletcher, LSDA
Stuart Gardner, LSC
Maggie Greenwood, LSDA
David Hargreaves, Visiting Professor, Roehampton University
Ingrid Schoon, City University

Expert seminar delegates

David Andrews, The National Institute for Careers Education and Counselling
Jude Belsham, CYPFD, DfES
Jan Bennett, Ofsted
Steve Besley, EDEXCEL
Lia Borgese, Social Exclusion Unit, DfES
Mike Cooper, LSDA
Peter Davies, LSDA
Mick Fletcher, LSDA
Stuart Gardner, LSC
Maggie Greenwood, LSDA
Nicholas Houghton, LSDA
John Jones, DfES
Kay Kinder, NFER
Janette King, DfES
Steven McIntosh, Centre for Economic Performance, London School of Economics
Charles Ritchie, DfES
Darshan Sachdev, LSDA
Hilary Steedman, Centre for Economic Performance, London School of Economics
Anna Vignoles, LSE
Judith Watson, University of Brighton
Sue Yeomans, LSC
Rosie Zwart, LSDA